SKINNY SUPPERS

SKINNY SUPPERS

COLLINS & BROWN

The Good Housekeeping website is
www.goodhousekeeping.co.uk

ISBN 978-1-909397-53-8

A catalogue record for this book is available from
the British Library.

Reproduction by Mission Productions Ltd,
Hong Kong
Printed and bound by 1010 Printing International Ltd,
China

This book can be ordered direct from the publisher.
Contact the marketing department, but try your
bookshop first.

www.anovabooks.com

NOTES

Both metric and imperial measures are given for
the recipes. Follow either set of measures, not a
mixture of both, as they are not interchangeable.

All spoon measures are level.
1 tsp = 5ml spoon; 1 tbsp = 15ml spoon.

Ovens and grills must be preheated to the specified
temperature.

Medium eggs should be used except where
otherwise specified. Free-range eggs are
recommended.

Note that some recipes contain raw or lightly
cooked eggs. The young, elderly, pregnant women
and anyone with an immune-deficiency disease
should avoid these because of the slight risk of
salmonella.

Contents

Light Bites

Make the Most of Your Calories

Calories are a measurement of energy, just as kilograms are a measurement of weight. Take in more calories than your body uses, and you'll gain weight. Use more calories than you take in, and you'll lose weight.

By selecting empty-calorie foods, you're spending a lot for something that offers very little – like some insanely expensive, very trendy shoes that give you blisters and are difficult to walk in.

If you're economizing on calories to lose weight, it makes sense to pack a lot of nutrition into what you eat. A food that's loaded with fibre, vitamins and minerals but also low in calories is a nutritional bargain – it's a nutrient-dense food.

On the other hand, foods such as fizzy drinks and sweets will load you with lots of calories and are low in vitamins and minerals, making them low-nutrient, calorie-dense foods. Such foods are often called 'empty-calorie' foods, but describing them as empty of nutrients would be more accurate. And remember, nutrient-dense foods will fill you up for far longer than calorie-dense foods.

This doesn't mean that chips, burgers, sweets and other less stellar choices are diet no-nos. The truth is that no food or drink is so high in calories, fat or sugar that including it on occasions in a diet that is healthy overall is going to sabotage your weight loss. Just be sure to keep your total calorie intake within the recommended limits (see page 82). Here's what to look for:

- **Fruits and vegetables** Rich in nutrients and low in calories, fruit and veg are a dieter's best friend. There's no such thing as a bad fruit or vegetable, but the more of a variety you eat, the better.
- **Low-fat dairy** These versions of milk, cheese, yogurt, cottage cheese, and so on, are packed with nutrition and have fewer calories than the regular versions.
- **Lean proteins** Lean meat, poultry and fish, as well as vegetarian choices such as beans and tofu, will help you feel full and stay that way.
- **Wholegrains** Select fibre-rich, wholegrain foods such as oatmeal, wholemeal bread and wholegrain rice instead of refined grains such as white bread, white pasta and white rice.
- **Healthy fats** Choose olive and rapeseed oils, avocados, nuts and nut butters, seeds and olives – but remember, a little goes a long, long way. A drizzle of olive oil on your salad, a small handful of nuts with your cereal, or a few slices of avocado on your sandwich all ensure satiety and flavour.

Full-of-goodness Soup

Hands-on time: 10 minutes
Cooking time: about 8 minutes

1–2 tbsp medium curry paste

200ml (7fl oz) reduced-fat coconut milk

600ml (1 pint) hot vegetable stock

200g (7oz) smoked tofu, cubed

2 pak choi, chopped

a handful of sugarsnap peas

4 spring onions, chopped

lime wedges to serve

1 Heat the curry paste in a pan for 1–2 minutes. Add the coconut milk and hot stock and bring to the boil.
2 Add the tofu, pak choi, sugarsnap peas and spring onions, then reduce the heat and simmer for 1–2 minutes.
3 Ladle into warmed bowls and serve each with a wedge of lime to squeeze over the soup.

Serves 4

Herb and Lemon Soup

Hands-on time: 10 minutes
Cooking time: 15 minutes

1.7 litres (3 pints) chicken stock
150g (5oz) orzo or other dried soup
  pasta
3 medium eggs
juice of 1 large lemon
2 tbsp finely chopped fresh chives
2 tbsp finely chopped fresh chervil
salt and freshly ground black pepper
lemon wedges to serve

1 Bring the stock to the boil in a large pan. Add the pasta and cook for 5 minutes or according to the pack instructions.

2 Beat the eggs in a bowl until frothy, then add the lemon juice and 1 tbsp cold water. Slowly stir in two ladlefuls of the hot stock. Put the egg mixture into the pan with the rest of the stock, then warm through over a very low heat for 2–3 minutes.

3 Add the chives and chervil and season with salt and ground black pepper. Ladle the soup into warmed bowls and serve immediately, with lemon wedges.

Serves 6

Panzanella Soup

Hands-on time: 20 minutes
Cooking time: about 15 minutes

1 red onion, finely chopped
2 garlic cloves, crushed
2 red peppers, seeded and roughly chopped
1 cucumber, peeled, halved lengthways, seeded and roughly chopped
1 tbsp olive oil, plus extra to garnish
125g (4oz) wholemeal bread, cut into 2cm (¾in) cubes
400g can chopped tomatoes
750ml (1¼ pints) vegetable stock
a large handful of fresh basil
salt and freshly ground black pepper

To serve (optional)
black olives, pitted and sliced
capers

1 Put the onion, garlic, red peppers and cucumber into a large pan with a splash of water. Cook gently until softened – about 10 minutes (add a little water as needed).

2 Meanwhile, heat the oil in a separate large frying pan over a low-medium heat. Add the bread cubes and some salt. Cook, tossing occasionally, until golden. Put to one side.

FREEZE AHEAD
To make ahead and freeze, prepare the soup to the end of step 3 (without making the croûtons). Cool, chill and pack into a freezer bag. Freeze for up to six months. To serve, thaw completely, then reheat gently in a pan. Make the croûtons and complete the recipe.

3 Add the tomatoes, stock, most of the basil and some seasoning to the vegetable pan. Simmer for 5 minutes, then whiz the soup in a blender or food processor and check the seasoning.

4 Reheat, if needed, and pour into four warmed bowls. Garnish, if you like, with the olives, capers, oil and remaining basil. Serve with the croûtons.

Kitchen Clean-up

To avoid temptation in your kitchen, donate unopened foods
on the list below to a local charity or use up what you have to hand,
then stock up on the must-have healthier options.

Items to avoid

Steer clear of high-calorie, nutrient-poor foods including:

- Crisps
- Salted nuts
- Chocolates and sweets
- Biscuits
- Sugary cereals
- Pastries
- Cakes
- White bread
- Creamy salad dressing and sauces
- Full-fat mayonnaise
- Cream
- Sausages and burgers
- Bacon, pancetta and lardons
- Cured meats such as salami and chorizo
- Canned meats
- Squash, fizzy drinks and juice drinks

Must-haves for your fridge

Add these fridge essentials to your weekly shopping list so that they are always to hand:

- **Seasonal fresh fruit and vegetables**
- **Cheese** – lower-fat cheeses such as Edam, feta and Gouda, or small amounts of full-fat strong cheeses such as mature Cheddar or Parmesan to provide a flavour lift.
- **Hummus**
- **Semi-skimmed or skimmed milk (or soya milk) and yogurt**
- **Eggs**
- **Fresh chicken, turkey and lean meat**

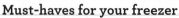

Must-haves for your freezer

A quick, healthy meal or treat is always just minutes away:

- **Healthy frozen ready meals**
- **Boneless, skinless chicken breasts and fish fillets** are easy everyday dinner solutions when paired with a quick sauce.
- **Bags of frozen fruits** (such as raspberries, mixed berries) and vegetables (such as spinach, peas).
- **Portions of home-made low-fat soups and casseroles**
- **Frozen yogurt**

Must-have condiments

Add low-calorie flavour with these extras:

- **Mustard** (wholegrain, Dijon, and so on).
- **Spray salad dressings**
- **Vinegar** (balsamic, sherry, red wine, white wine, and so on).
- **Oils** (good options include olive, rapeseed, safflower and flaxseed oils).
- **Herbs and spices,** fresh and dried.

Must-haves for your food cupboard

Once you've cleaned out the shelves, it's time to fill them with healthy options:

- **Wholegrains** such as wholewheat pasta, wholegrain rice and noodles.
- **Low-fat sauces** such as pasta sauce, salsa, and so on.
- **Wholemeal bread**, wraps, rolls, pitta breads, tortillas, and so on.
- **Beans and pulses**
- **Healthy canned items** (such as beans and pulses, salmon and tuna in water, tomatoes, low-fat soups and fruit in juice).
- **Nuts, seeds and occasional treats**

Look for unsweetened choices

It's easy to pick up a jar of pasta sauce, a carton of soup or a pack of breakfast cereal without realizing that a lot of sugar has been added. One leading fresh soup, for example, has 6 teaspoons of sugar in a 600ml (1 pint) carton, while a pasta sauce from another manufacturer has 6½ teaspoons in a 500g (1lb 2oz) jar. For foods like these, which often taste great without being sweetened, be sure to check the ingredients list and look for unsweetened or only slightly sweetened alternatives.

Spice up your meals

Research has shown that spicy flavours can have long-lasting weight-reduction benefits; for example capsaicin, a compound found in chillies and cayenne pepper, can be a powerful appetite suppressant, metabolism booster and fat burner. A Canadian study found that people who ate appetizers made with chillies consumed 189 fewer calories at their next meal. Not a fan of spicy foods? Zero-calorie herbs are also a great way to punch up the flavour in a dish.

Go brown

Replacing white products with wholegrain versions could help you lose those pounds, say Danish scientists. Overweight women on a 1,250-calorie diet were asked to include either 480 calories of refined grain foods or the same amount of wholegrain foods. Those eating the diet with wholegrains lost 3.6kg (8lb) – about 1kg (2¼lb) more weight and significantly more body fat after 12 weeks, compared to those eating refined grains.

Make it with mushrooms

Replace beef with mushrooms in lasagne and spaghetti bolognese and you'll eat about 420 fewer calories. People in a 2008 US study said the mushroom makeovers tasted just as good and kept them feeling full for just as long as the beef versions did. And not only did the mushroom-based dish mean a lower-calorie meal, but the mushroom-eaters also ate fewer calories and less fat throughout the day than the beef-eaters.

Eat more fish

Follow a low-calorie diet that includes more fish than meat and the chances are that you'll drop more pounds than you would otherwise – at least, that's according to a study published in the International Journal of Obesity. One possible explanation is that, gram for gram, fish has fewer calories than almost all cuts of beef, pork and skin-on poultry. Researchers theorize that omega-3 fatty acids, the polyunsaturated fats abundant in cold-water fish such as salmon and mackerel, switch on the fat-burning process in cells – provided that you also exercise.

Sprouted Bean and Mango Salad

Hands-on time: 15 minutes

3 tbsp mango chutney

grated zest and juice of 1 lime

2 tbsp olive oil

4 plum tomatoes

1 small red onion, chopped

1 red pepper, seeded and finely diced

1 yellow pepper, seeded and finely diced

1 mango, peeled, stoned and finely diced (see page 145)

4 tbsp freshly chopped coriander

150g (5oz) sprouted beans (see Save Money)

salt and freshly ground black pepper

1 To make the dressing, place the mango chutney in a small bowl and add the lime zest and juice. Whisk in the oil and season with salt and ground black pepper.

2 Quarter the tomatoes, discard the seeds and then cut into dice. Put into a large bowl with the onion, peppers, mango, coriander and sprouted beans. Pour the dressing over and mix well. Serve the salad immediately.

SAVE MONEY

Many beans and seeds can be sprouted at home, but buy ones that are specifically produced for sprouting. Mung beans take five to six days to sprout. Allow 125g (4oz) bean sprouts per person.

Serves 6

Beetroot and Bulgur Wheat Salad

Hands-on time: 15 minutes
Cooking time: about 30 minutes

2 red onions, each cut into 8 wedges

2 medium beetroot (total weight about 300g/11oz), peeled and cut into wedges

1 tbsp olive oil, plus extra to drizzle (optional)

200g (7oz) bulgur wheat

350ml (12fl oz) vegetable or chicken stock

200g (7oz) frozen soya beans or peas

juice of 1 lemon

100g (3½oz) feta, crumbled

a large handful of fresh mint, roughly chopped

100g (3½oz) spinach leaves

salt and freshly ground black pepper

1 Preheat the oven to 200°C (180°C fan oven) mark 6. Put the onions and beetroot wedges on a baking tray, add the oil, then season well and gently toss together. Roast for 25–30 minutes until tender.

2 Meanwhile, toast the bulgur wheat in a medium pan over a medium heat for 2 minutes to bring out its nutty flavour. Carefully pour in the stock (it will bubble wildly). Simmer for 5 minutes, then add the soya beans or peas and continue cooking for 3 minutes. Leave for 10 minutes to cool slightly, then fork through the mixture to loosen and fluff it up. Stir in the lemon juice, feta, mint and spinach leaves and check the seasoning.

3 Divide the bulgur mixture among four serving plates. Top each with some of the roasted vegetables and drizzle some extra oil over, if you like.

Serves 4

Falafel, Rocket and Soured Cream Wraps

Hands-on time: 5 minutes, plus chilling

6 large flour tortillas
200g (7oz) soured cream
100g (3½oz) wild rocket
a small handful of fresh coriander, chopped
1 celery stick, finely chopped
180g pack of ready-made falafel, roughly chopped or crumbled

1 Lay the tortillas on a board and spread each one with a little soured cream.
2 Divide the rocket among the wraps and sprinkle with coriander, celery and falafel.
3 Roll up as tightly as you can, then wrap each roll in clingfilm and chill for up to 3 hours or until ready to use. To serve, unwrap and cut each roll into quarters.

Serves 6

Simple Seafood Sushi

Hands-on time: 20 minutes
Cooking time: about 15 minutes, plus cooling and chilling

150g (5oz) shortgrain rice, unwashed
100g (3½oz) white crab meat
100g (3½oz) small cooked prawns, finely chopped
1 avocado, stoned and finely chopped
1 red pepper, seeded and finely chopped
2 tbsp extra light mayonnaise
2 tbsp mirin rice wine
½ tbsp sesame seeds
4 sheets dried seaweed, each about 19 × 22cm (7½ × 8½in)
salt and freshly ground black pepper

To serve
pickled ginger (optional)
wasabi (optional)
soy sauce (optional)
green salad

1 Put the unwashed rice into a pan, cover well with cold water and bring to the boil. Reduce the heat and simmer for 15 minutes, then drain. Tip into a large bowl and leave to cool completely.

2 Stir the crab, prawns, avocado, pepper, mayonnaise, mirin, sesame seeds and some seasoning into the cooled rice.

3 Put a sheet of seaweed on a large piece of clingfilm. Spread one quarter of the rice mixture along one edge, then roll up as tightly as possible and wrap well in the clingfilm. Repeat the process three times. Chill the rolls for 15 minutes to allow the seaweed to soften.

4 To serve, remove the clingfilm and cut each roll in half on a diagonal. Serve with pickled ginger, wasabi and soy sauce, if you like, plus a green salad.

Serves 4

Sardines on Toast

Hands-on time: 5 minutes
Cooking time: about 10 minutes

4 thick slices wholemeal bread

2 large tomatoes, sliced

2 × 120g cans sardines in olive oil,
    drained

juice of ½ lemon

freshly ground black pepper

a small handful of fresh parsley,
    chopped, to garnish

1 Preheat the grill. Toast the bread on both sides.

2 Divide the tomato slices and the sardines among the toast slices, squeeze the lemon juice over them, then put back under the grill for 2–3 minutes to heat through. Season with ground black pepper, then scatter the parsley over the sardines to garnish and serve immediately.

Serves 4

Mozzarella Mushrooms

Hands-on time: 5 minutes
Cooking time: about 20 minutes

8 large portabello mushrooms
8 slices marinated red pepper
8 fresh basil leaves
150g (5oz) mozzarella cheese, cut into
   8 slices
4 English muffins, halved
salt and freshly ground black pepper
green salad to serve

HEALTHY TIP

Mushrooms are an excellent source of potassium – a mineral that helps lower elevated blood pressure and reduces the risk of stroke. One medium portabello mushroom has even more potassium than a banana or a glass of orange juice. Mushrooms contain antioxidant nutrients that can help to inhibit the development of cancers of the breast and prostate.

1 Preheat the oven to 200°C (180°C fan oven) mark 6. Lay the mushrooms side by side in a roasting tin and season with salt and ground black pepper. Top each mushroom with a slice of red pepper and a basil leaf. Lay a slice of mozzarella on top of each mushroom and season again. Roast for 15–20 minutes until the mushrooms are tender and the cheese has melted.

2 Meanwhile, toast the muffin halves until golden. Put a mozzarella mushroom on top of each muffin half. Serve immediately with a green salad.

Serves 4

Cheesy Polenta with Tomato Sauce

Hands-on time: 15 minutes
Cooking time: about 40 minutes, plus cooling

a little vegetable oil

225g (8oz) polenta

4 tbsp freshly chopped herbs, such as oregano, chives and flat-leafed parsley

100g (3½oz) freshly grated Parmesan, plus Parmesan shavings to serve

salt and freshly ground black pepper

For the tomato and basil sauce

1 tbsp vegetable oil

3 garlic cloves, crushed

500g carton creamed tomatoes or passata

1 bay leaf

1 fresh thyme sprig

a large pinch of caster sugar

3 tbsp freshly chopped basil, plus extra to garnish

1 Lightly oil a 25.5 × 18cm (10 × 7in) dish. Bring 1.1 litres (2 pints) water and ¼ tsp salt to the boil in a large pan. Sprinkle in the polenta, whisking constantly. Reduce the heat and simmer, stirring frequently, for 10–15 minutes until the mixture leaves the sides of the pan.

2 Stir in the herbs and Parmesan and season to taste with salt and ground black pepper. Turn into the prepared dish and leave to cool.

3 Next, make the tomato and basil sauce. Heat the oil in a pan, add the garlic and fry for 30 seconds (do not brown). Add the creamed tomatoes or passata, the bay leaf, thyme and sugar. Season with salt and ground black pepper and bring to the boil, then reduce the heat and simmer, uncovered, for 5–10 minutes. Remove the bay leaf and thyme sprig and add the chopped basil.

Serves 6

4 To serve, preheat a griddle or grill. Cut the polenta into pieces and lightly brush with oil. Fry on the hot griddle for 3-4 minutes on each side, or under the hot grill for 7-8 minutes on each side. Serve with the tomato and basil sauce, Parmesan shavings and chopped basil.

SAVE TIME

To prepare ahead, complete the recipe to the end of step 3. Cover and chill separately for up to two days. Complete the recipe to serve.

Midweek
Suppers

Detox your kitchen

Clear your cupboards, fridge and freezer of the foods you know will get you into trouble, and instead stock up on healthy and tasty options you and your family will enjoy. Conduct your own in-house taste tests – ask your family to get involved, try new, lower-calorie recipes and new foods, and gain a new (and healthy) weight-loss perspective.

Recipe makeovers

Substitute ingredients used in everyday cooking with healthier options and you'll slash calories. The cooking tricks below will not only help you maintain your desired weight once you get there, but are useful things for all the family to learn.

Here are some tips for trimming excess fat and calories from home-cooked meals:

- Choose lean cuts of meat and trim all visible fat before cooking. Remove the skin from poultry before or after cooking.
- Cut back on the fat in proper gravy – just pour most of the fat out of the used roasting tin before you make gravy. Alternatively, invest in a gravy separator, which will split the fat from the meat juices so that you can pour a sin-free version over your Sunday roast.

- If a roast chicken tops your Sunday wish-list, rather than slathering it with butter before cooking, squeeze some lemon juice over the bird and drizzle with 1 tbsp olive oil. And when the chicken's cooked, remember to remove the skin before eating, as it is very fatty.
- A classic fore-rib of beef is high in fat – an artery-clogging 20g (¾oz) fat per 100g (3½oz). So opt for a leaner topside joint. Before roasting, sit the meat on a rack to allow much of the fat to drip into the tin during cooking, rather than leaving the meat swimming in it.
- Make skinny chips by slicing 2 large potatoes into wedges, then put them on a non-stick baking tray. Pour ½ tbsp olive oil over them, season and cook at 200°C (180°C fan oven) mark 6 for 30 minutes.
- Substitute protein-packed canned pulses, such as beans and lentils, for meat in casseroles; the dish will have fewer calories and more filling fibre.
- Use skimmed milk in a cheese sauce rather than whole milk, and replace ordinary Cheddar cheese with fuller-flavoured mature or vintage Cheddar – this will allow you to cut the amount of cheese you use by half.
- Be sparing with fat. Use non-stick pans or a non-stick cooking spray with regular pans.
- Experiment with fat-free flavourings: squeeze orange or lemon juice into stews; add citrus zest, soy sauce, fresh ginger, chilli peppers, herbs or tomato purée to your favourite recipes.
- Before roasting fish or chicken, spritz with olive oil spray before seasoning and adding herbs or spices, to minimize fat and maximize the taste of the flavourings. Spray oil on vegetables (rather than brushing it on) to cut down on fat.
- Turn potato salad into a healthy energy booster by replacing ordinary mayonnaise with 2 tbsp reduced-calorie mayonnaise mixed with an equal amount of low-fat natural yogurt.

- For a healthier version of spag bol, swap regular minced beef, at 15g (½oz) fat per 100g (3½oz), for extra-lean mince, at 10g (¼oz) fat per 100g (3½oz), or turkey mince, at 7g (¼oz) fat per 100g (3½oz), then brown in a little oil. Add flavour with fresh herbs and boost the nutritional value with celery, mushrooms and carrots.
- Swap double cream in sauces for low-fat natural yogurt to dramatically lower the fat content of a dish. Take care not to let the sauce boil, though, as this might cause it to split.

Downsize your dishes

Use smaller plates and glasses for everyday meals. According to a Cornell University study, people tend to serve themselves 30% more food when given large bowls and spoons. And research at the Food and Brand Lab at the University of Illinois found that people who used short, wide glasses poured 76% more soda, milk or juice than when they used tall, slender ones.

No need to buy new, though: simply swap your dinner plate for a side plate or salad plate, or a large glass for a small glass. Or, if you have fashionably oversized dishes and glasses, use a measuring jug or measuring cups to familiarize yourself with calorie-controlled portions and keep these studies in mind as you ladle out the servings.

Control cravings

Whether it's chocolate or chips, ice cream or whipped cream, the foods people crave have one thing in common – they are calorie-dense, a Tufts University study recently confirmed. But, in that study, the researchers also noted that while virtually everyone had cravings, the dieters in the group who successfully lost weight or kept it off gave in to their must-haves – but just less often.

Pay attention

A recent study showed that Americans (and the British are much the same) use external cues, such as waiting until their television programme is over, to stop eating, unlike the don't-get-fat French, who rely on internal messages, such as feeling full. We're also susceptible to social influences. Many of us keep eating until almost everyone at the table is finished. If you tend to finish before your family, keep the salad bowl in front of you to pick from, rather than having extra pasta and sauce.

One-pan Chicken with Tomatoes

Hands-on time: 5 minutes
Cooking time: about 25 minutes

4 chicken thighs

1 red onion, sliced

400g can chopped tomatoes with herbs

400g can mixed beans, drained and rinsed

2 tsp balsamic vinegar

freshly chopped flat-leafed parsley to garnish

1 Heat a non-stick pan and fry the chicken thighs, skin side down, until golden. Turn over and fry for 5 minutes.

2 Add the onion and fry for 5 minutes. Add the tomatoes, mixed beans and vinegar, cover and simmer for 10–12 minutes until piping hot. Garnish with chopped parsley and serve immediately.

Serves 4

Chicken with Spicy Couscous

Hands-on time: 15 minutes, plus soaking

125g (4oz) couscous

1 ripe mango, peeled, stoned and
   cut into 2.5cm (1in) chunks
   (see page 145)

1 tbsp lemon or lime juice

125g tub fresh tomato salsa

3 tbsp mango chutney

3 tbsp orange juice

2 tbsp freshly chopped coriander, plus
   extra to garnish

200g (7oz) chargrilled chicken fillets

4 tbsp fromage frais (optional)

salt and freshly ground black pepper

lime wedges to garnish

1 Put the couscous into a large bowl
  and pour 300ml (½ pint) boiling
  water over. Season well with salt and
  ground black pepper, then leave to
  soak for 15 minutes.

2 Put the mango chunks on a large
  plate and sprinkle with the lemon or
  lime juice.

3 Mix the tomato salsa with the
  mango chutney, orange juice and
  coriander in a small bowl.

4 Drain the couscous if necessary,
  fluff the grains with a fork, then
  stir in the salsa mixture and check
  the seasoning. Turn out on to a
  large serving dish and arrange the
  chicken and mango on top.

5 Just before serving, spoon the
  fromage frais over the chicken, if
  you like, then garnish with extra
  chopped coriander and some
  lime wedges.

HEALTHY TIP

Couscous is made from
semolina flour and has a low
GI (glycaemic index), helping
to make you feel fuller longer.
It provides B vitamins and
valuable amounts of selenium.
Mango is rich in betacarotene,
an antioxidant that helps combat
harmful free radicals and
promotes healthy skin.

Serves 4

Zesty Turkey One-pan

Hands-on time: 10 minutes
Cooking time: about 10 minutes

½ tbsp olive oil

4 turkey breast steaks, (total weight about 500g/1lb 2oz)

350ml (12fl oz) chicken stock

grated zest and juice of 2 lemons

25g (1oz) capers, rinsed and chopped

4 tomatoes, roughly chopped

a large handful of fresh curly parsley, roughly chopped

salt and freshly ground black pepper

boiled rice, seasonal vegetables or salad to serve

1 Heat the oil in a large frying pan over a high heat, add the turkey steaks and fry for 2 minutes, turning once to brown the steaks. Add the stock, lemon zest and juice, the capers, tomatoes and some seasoning. Simmer for 8 minutes or until the turkey is cooked through.

2 Add the parsley and check the seasoning. Serve with boiled rice, seasonal vegetables or salad.

Serves 4

Perfect Stir-fry

Stir-frying is a healthy and speedy way to cook poultry and other tender cuts of meat. It's also perfect for non-starchy vegetables, as the quick cooking preserves their colour, freshness and texture.

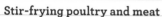

Stir-frying poultry and meat

1 Trim off any fat, then cut the poultry or meat into even-size strips or dice no more than 5mm (¼in) thick. Heat a wok or large pan until hot and add oil to coat the inside.

2 Add the poultry or meat and cook, stirring constantly, until just done. Remove and put to one side. Cook the other ingredients you are using for the stir-fry, then put the poultry or meat back into the pan and cook for 1–2 minutes to heat through.

HEALTHY TIP

Stir-frying in a wok uses less fat than other frying techniques, and cooking briefly over a high heat retains as many nutrients as possible.

Stir-frying Vegetables

- Cut everything into small pieces of uniform size so that they cook quickly and evenly.
- If you're cooking onions or garlic with the vegetables, don't keep them in the high heat for too long or they will burn.
- Add liquids towards the end of cooking so they don't evaporate.

You will need 450g (1lb) vegetables, 1–2 tbsp vegetable oil, 2 crushed garlic cloves, 2 tbsp soy sauce, 2 tsp sesame oil.

1 Cut the vegetables into even-size pieces. Heat the oil in a large wok or frying pan until smoking-hot. Add the garlic and cook for a few seconds, then remove and put to one side.

2 Add the vegetables to the wok, then toss and stir them. Keep them moving constantly as they cook, which will take 4–5 minutes.

3 When the vegetables are just tender, but still with a slight bite, turn off the heat. Put the garlic back into the wok and stir well. Add the soy sauce and sesame oil, toss and serve.

Quick Turkey and Pork Stir-fry

Hands-on time: 15 minutes
Cooking time: about 10 minutes

1 tbsp vegetable oil
200g (7oz) turkey breast, cut into
   finger-size strips
200g (7oz) pork loin fillet, cut into
   finger-size strips
1 tbsp Chinese five-spice powder
1 each yellow and orange pepper,
   seeded and sliced
150g (5oz) pak choi, thickly shredded
1 tsp sesame seeds
1–1½ tbsp soy sauce, to taste
a large handful of fresh coriander
salt and freshly ground black pepper
boiled rice or cooked noodles to serve
   (optional)

1 Heat the oil in a large wok or frying pan over a high heat, add the turkey and pork and cook for 3 minutes, stirring occasionally.

2 Add the five-spice powder, sliced peppers, pak choi and a splash of water and cook for a few minutes until the vegetables are just tender (but retaining a crunch) and the meat is cooked through (add more water as needed).

3 Sprinkle the sesame seeds over, add the soy sauce and rip in the coriander. Check the seasoning and serve with rice or noodles, if you like.

Steak and Asparagus Stir-fry

🍴 **Hands-on time:** 10 minutes, plus marinating
Cooking time: about 10 minutes

1 × 225g (8oz) rump steak, trimmed and sliced
2 tbsp runny honey
2 tbsp teriyaki sauce
1 tbsp sesame oil
150g (5oz) tenderstem broccoli, cut into 5cm (2in) lengths
150g (5oz) asparagus, cut into 5cm (2in) lengths
75g (3oz) water chestnuts
1 tbsp sesame seeds
salt and freshly ground black pepper
boiled brown rice to serve

1 Put the steak, honey, teriyaki sauce and sesame oil into a bowl. Stir and leave to marinate for 5 minutes.

2 Heat a wok over a high heat. Lift the beef out of the marinade (keeping the mixture to one side) and stir-fry for 3 minutes or until caramelized and cooked to medium (cook for longer or shorter, if you like). Empty the beef into a clean bowl and put to one side.

3 Put the wok back on the heat and add the broccoli, asparagus and a splash of water. Fry for 3 minutes or until the vegetables are just tender. Stir in the marinade, water chestnuts and beef and heat for 30 seconds. Check the seasoning. Sprinkle the sesame seeds over and serve immediately with boiled brown rice.

HEALTHY TIP

Sesame seeds are deliciously nutty and highly nutritious. They are a valuable source of protein, good omega fats and vitamin E.

Serves 4

Fast Fish Soup

Hands-on time: 5 minutes
Cooking time: about 15 minutes

1 onion, chopped
1 fennel bulb, roughly chopped
1 tbsp vegetable oil
400g can chopped tomatoes
500ml (17fl oz) fish stock
1 bay leaf
finely grated zest of 1 lemon
300g (11oz) smoked haddock or
   smoked cod, diced
a large handful of parsley, freshly
   chopped
salt and freshly ground black pepper

1 Pulse the onion and fennel in a food processor until pea size. Heat the oil in a large pan, add the chopped vegetables and fry over a medium heat for 10 minutes or until soft. Add the tomatoes, stock, bay leaf and lemon zest.

2 Bring to the boil, then add the fish and cook for 2–3 minutes until the fish is cooked and opaque. Season with salt and ground black pepper. Remove the bay leaf, stir in the parsley and serve.

Cod with Cherry Tomatoes

Hands-on time: 15 minutes
Cooking time: about 25 minutes

4 × 100g (3½oz) cod steaks
1 tbsp plain flour
2 tbsp olive oil
1 small onion, sliced
1 large red chilli, seeded and chopped
1 garlic clove, crushed
250g (9oz) cherry tomatoes, halved
4 spring onions, chopped
2 tbsp freshly chopped coriander
salt and freshly ground black pepper

1 Season the cod with salt and ground black pepper, then dust lightly with the flour. Heat 1 tbsp of the oil in a large frying pan over a medium heat. Add the onion and fry gently for 5–10 minutes until golden.

2 Pour the remaining oil into the pan. Add the cod and fry for 3 minutes on each side. Add the chilli, garlic, cherry tomatoes, spring onions and coriander and season with salt and ground black pepper. Cover and continue to cook for 5–10 minutes until everything is heated through. Serve immediately.

Serves 4

Steamed Fish and Vegetable Parcels

Hands-on time: 15 minutes
Cooking time: about 20 minutes

1 lemon

40g (1½oz) butter, softened

400g can cannellini beans, drained and rinsed

1 fennel bulb, thinly sliced

1 courgette, peeled into ribbons

4 × 125g (4oz) boneless, skinless white fish fillets, such as haddock, pollack or coley

8 small fresh dill sprigs

salt and freshly ground black pepper

green salad and crusty bread to serve

1 Preheat the oven to 200°C (180°C fan oven) mark 6. Cut four rough 38cm (15in) squares of baking parchment.

2 Grate the zest from the lemon, then put it into a small bowl with the butter and plenty of seasoning. Stir to combine, then put to one side. Slice the zested lemon into thin rounds.

3 On one half of each square, pile a quarter of each of the beans, fennel and courgette. Top each pile with a fish fillet, then top with some lemon slices. Dollop a quarter of the butter on to each pile of vegetables and fish, then add the dill sprigs and some seasoning. Spoon 2 tbsp water on to each pile. Seal the parcels by pulling the paper up and over the filling, then folding the edges.

4 Put the parcels on baking sheets and cook in the oven for 18-20 minutes. To test whether the fish is cooked without opening the parcel, press the fish gently through the paper – it should feel as if it is flaking. Transfer the parcels to plates and bring to the table with some salad, and bread to mop up the juices.

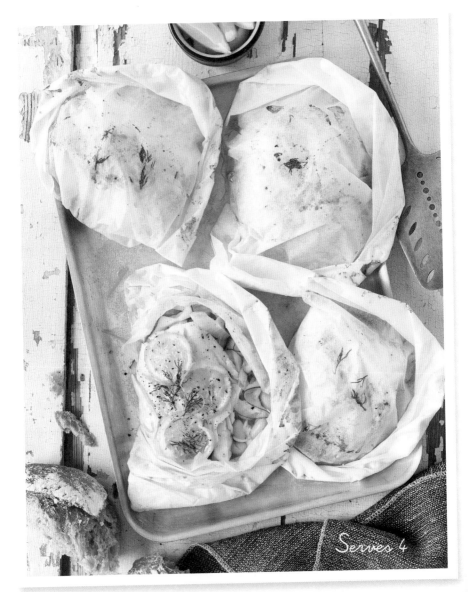

Serves 4

Huevos Rancheros

Hands-on time: 10 minutes
Cooking time: about 15 minutes

1 tbsp vegetable oil

1 medium red onion, finely sliced

1 each yellow and red pepper, seeded
   and finely sliced

1 red chilli, seeded and finely sliced

2 × 400g cans chopped tomatoes

½ tsp dried mixed herbs

4 large eggs

a small handful of fresh flat-leafed
   parsley, roughly chopped

salt and freshly ground black pepper

crusty bread to serve

1 Heat the oil in a large frying pan over a high heat. Add the onion, peppers and chilli and fry for 3 minutes or until just softened. Add the tomatoes and dried herbs. Season with salt and ground black pepper and simmer for 3 minutes.

2 Break an egg into a small cup. Use a wooden spoon to scrape a hole in the tomato mixture, then quickly drop in the egg. Repeat with the remaining eggs, spacing them evenly around the tomato mixture. Cover the pan and simmer for 3–5 minutes until the eggs are just set. Sprinkle with parsley and serve with crusty bread.

Serves 6

Oriental Baked Tofu

Hands-on time: 5 minutes
Cooking time: 15 minutes

150g (5oz) firm tofu
½ garlic clove, thinly sliced
2cm (¾in) piece fresh root ginger,
   peeled and cut into matchsticks
1 tsp soy sauce
a small handful of fresh coriander
a few chilli rings
freshly ground black pepper
lime wedges to serve

1 Preheat the oven to 220°C (200°C fan oven) mark 7. Stack two 30.5cm (12in) sheets of greaseproof paper, baking parchment or foil and put the tofu on top.
2 Sprinkle the garlic slices, ginger, soy sauce and some ground black pepper on top. Fold the paper, parchment or foil over, then fold in the edges to seal.
3 Put the parcel on a baking sheet and cook in the oven for 15 minutes. Open the parcel and sprinkle in the coriander and a few chilli rings. Serve with lime wedges.

SAVE TIME

To prepare ahead, assemble the parcel and put on a baking sheet (do not cook) up to 3 hours ahead. Chill. Complete the recipe to serve.

Serves 1

Low-cal Comfort

Of all the nutrients in our diet, fat must be the most debated and the most misunderstood. Although in terms of healthy eating, fat is often cast as the villain, it's worth remembering that it also plays a beneficial role. In the body, fat cushions and protects the vital organs, provides energy stores and helps insulate the body. In the diet, it is necessary for the absorption of fat-soluble vitamins (A, D, E and K) and to provide essential fatty acids that the body can't make itself. While some fat is essential, many of us are eating too much of the wrong types of fat and not enough of the right types. A high-fat diet, particularly one that contains a lot of saturated 'animal' fats, is known to increase the risk of problems such as heart disease, stroke and certain types of cancer. There are three types of fat: saturated, monounsaturated and polyunsaturated fatty acids,

which occur in different proportions in foods. Saturated fatty acids are linked to higher blood cholesterol, which can then lead to heart disease.

Polyunsaturated fats
Omega-6 fats These are mostly found in vegetable oils and margarines such as sunflower oil, safflower oil, corn oil and soya bean oil. Omega-6 fats help lower the LDL ('bad') cholesterol in the blood, but if you eat too much they will also lower the 'good'.

HDL cholesterol
Omega-3 fats These are found mainly in oil-rich fish such as salmon, fresh tuna, mackerel and sardines, in linseeds (flax) and rapeseed oil. They help to protect the heart by making the blood less sticky and likely to clot, by lowering blood pressure, and by encouraging the muscles lining the artery walls

to relax, thus improving blood flow to the heart. It's important to have a balance of omega-3 and omega-6 fats in the diet. Most of us have too many omega-6 fats and not enough omega-3 fats and recent research suggests that low levels of omega-3s in the blood may contribute to depression, antisocial behaviour and schizophrenia.

Monounsaturated fats

Monounsaturated fats are found mainly in olive oil, walnut oil and rapeseed oil, nuts and avocados. They can help reduce the risk of heart disease by lowering LDL ('bad') cholesterol.

Saturated fats

Saturated 'animal' fats are found in full-fat dairy products (cheese, yogurt, milk, cream), lard, fatty cuts of meat and meat products such as sausages and burgers, pastry, cakes, biscuits, and coconut and palm oil. A diet high in saturated fats can raise levels of LDL ('bad') cholesterol in the blood, which will cause narrowing of the arteries and increase the risk of heart attacks and stroke.

Trans fats

Trans fats occur naturally in small amounts in meat and dairy products, but they are also produced during the process of hydrogenation that is used to convert liquid vegetable oils into semi-solid fats in the manufacture of some types of margarine. Trans fats are most commonly found in biscuits, cakes, pastries, meat pies, sausages, crackers and takeaway foods. Although, chemically, trans fats are still unsaturated fat, studies show that in the body they behave like saturated fat, causing blood cholesterol levels to rise; in fact, some studies suggest that trans fats are worse than saturated fats.

Chicken Tarragon Burgers

Hands-on time: 20 minutes, plus chilling
Cooking time: about 12 minutes

225g (8oz) minced chicken
2 shallots, finely chopped
1 tbsp freshly chopped tarragon
25g (1oz) fresh breadcrumbs
1 large egg yolk
vegetable oil
salt and freshly ground black pepper
toasted burger buns, mayonnaise
   or Greek yogurt, salad leaves and
   tomato salad to serve

1 Put the chicken into a bowl with the shallots, tarragon, breadcrumbs and egg yolk. Mix well, then beat in about 75ml (2½fl oz) cold water and season with salt and ground black pepper.

2 Lightly oil a foil-lined baking sheet. Divide the chicken mixture into two or four portions (depending on how large you want the burgers) and put on the foil. Using the back of a wet spoon, flatten each portion to a thickness of 2.5cm (1in). Cover and chill for 30 minutes.

3 Preheat the barbecue or grill. If cooking on the barbecue, lift the burgers straight on to the grill rack; if cooking under the grill, slide the baking sheet under the grill. Cook the burgers for 5–6 minutes on each side until they are cooked through, then serve in a toasted burger bun with a dollop of mayonnaise or Greek yogurt, a few salad leaves and tomato salad.

Turkey Meatballs with Barbecue Sauce

Hands-on time: 15 minutes
Cooking time: about 20 minutes

500g (1lb 2oz) turkey mince
2 tsp ground coriander
½–1 red chilli, seeded and finely chopped
½ tbsp olive oil
1 onion, finely chopped
1 garlic clove, crushed
400g can chopped tomatoes
2 tbsp soy sauce
3 tbsp tomato ketchup
salt and freshly ground black pepper
fresh coriander, chives or parsley to garnish
boiled wholegrain rice to serve

1 Preheat the oven to 200°C (180°C fan oven) mark 6 and line a baking tray with baking parchment.
2 Put the turkey mince into a large bowl, add the ground coriander, chilli and plenty of seasoning and mix through (using your hands is easiest). Form into walnut-sized meatballs – you should have about 20.
3 Arrange the meatballs on the prepared tray and cook in the oven, turning midway, for 20 minutes or until golden and cooked through.
4 Meanwhile, heat the oil in a large pan over a medium heat. Add the onion and fry for 10 minutes or until softened. Stir in the garlic and cook for 1 minute, then add the tomatoes, soy sauce, ketchup and seasoning. Bring to the boil, then reduce the heat and simmer for 10 minutes or until thickened slightly.
5 Add the meatballs to the sauce and stir gently to coat. Garnish with fresh herbs and serve with boiled wholegrain rice.

Serves 4

Turkey Breast with Fiery Honey Sauce

Hands-on time: 15 minutes
Cooking time: about 15 minutes

½ tbsp olive oil

4 turkey breast steaks (total weight about 500g/1lb 2oz)

1 tbsp Worcestershire sauce

½–1 red chilli, to taste, seeded and finely chopped

1½ tbsp runny honey

100ml (3½fl oz) chicken stock

4 spring onions, finely sliced

salt and freshly ground black pepper

seasonal vegetables, cooked noodles or salad to serve

1 Heat the oil in a large frying pan over a medium–high heat and cook the turkey steaks for 8-10 minutes, turning once, until cooked through. Transfer to a board, cover well with foil to keep warm and leave to rest while you prepare the sauce.

2 Put the pan back on the heat and add the Worcestershire sauce, chilli, honey, stock, spring onions and some seasoning. Heat through and leave to bubble for 2 minutes or until slightly thickened.

3 Serve the turkey and sauce with some seasonal vegetables, cooked noodles or salad.

HEALTHY TIP

Lean and low in fat, turkey is a good source of protein.

Serves 4

Chilli Beef Noodle Salad

Hands-on time: 15 minutes, plus soaking

150g (5oz) dried rice noodles

50g (2oz) rocket

125g (4oz) sliced cold roast beef

125g (4oz) sunblush tomatoes, chopped

For the Thai dressing

juice of 1 lime

1 lemongrass stalk, outside leaves discarded, trimmed and finely chopped

1 red chilli, seeded and chopped

2 tsp finely chopped fresh root ginger

2 garlic cloves, crushed

1 tbsp Thai fish sauce

3 tbsp extra virgin olive oil

salt and freshly ground black pepper

1 Put the noodles into a large bowl and pour boiling water over them to cover. Put to one side for 15 minutes.

2 To make the dressing, whisk together the lime juice, lemongrass, chilli, ginger, garlic, fish sauce and oil in a small bowl and season with salt and ground black pepper.

3 While they are still warm, drain the noodles well, put into a large bowl and toss with the dressing. Leave to cool.

4 Just before serving, toss the rocket, sliced beef and tomatoes through the noodles.

Understanding Salt

Reducing the amount of salt in our diet is, say health experts, one of the most important steps we can take to reduce the risk of high blood pressure, a condition that affects one in three adults in the UK.

The 2013 target of the Consensus Action on Salt and Health group is to reduce salt intake to an average of 6g a day for adults and even less for children. This reduction would have a big impact on reducing strokes by approximately 22% and heart attacks by 16% – saving 17,000 lives in the UK.

Hidden salt

You may think the easiest way to cut back on salt is not to sprinkle salt over your food when you're at the table, but unfortunately the answer isn't quite that simple – only about 15% of the salt we eat comes from salt added to our food during cooking and at the table. Three-quarters of all the salt we consume is hidden in processed foods – one small can of chicken soup, for instance, can contain well over half the recommended daily intake of salt for an adult.

Re-educating our taste buds

Our taste for salt is something we learn to like the more we eat. But just in the same way that we can teach our taste buds to enjoy foods with less sugar, we can train them to enjoy foods with less salt (sodium chloride). If you gradually reduce the amount of salt you eat, the taste receptors on the tongue become more sensitive to salt. This process takes between two and three weeks. Use herbs and spices to enhance the natural flavours of foods and before long you'll be enjoying the real taste of food – not the flavour of salt.

Healthy Fish Chowder

Hands-on time: 20 minutes
Cooking time: about 25 minutes

1 tbsp olive oil

1 onion, finely chopped

1 celery stick, finely chopped

500ml (17fl oz) hot fish or vegetable
   stock

250ml (9fl oz) skimmed milk

200g (7oz) baby new potatoes, halved

150g (5oz) skinless smoked haddock,
   diced

150g (5oz) skinless white fish, such as
   cod or pollack, diced

2 × 198g cans sweetcorn, drained

2 tbsp double cream

2 tbsp freshly chopped chives

salt and freshly ground black pepper

1 Heat the oil in a large pan over a medium heat. Add the onion and celery and gently fry until soft and translucent – about 10 minutes.

2 Add the hot stock and milk, then bring to the boil. Add the potatoes, then reduce the heat and simmer for about 10 minutes until the vegetables are tender.

3 Stir in the fish, sweetcorn and some seasoning and simmer until the fish is cooked – about 3–5 minutes. Carefully stir through the cream and most of the chives, then check the seasoning. Garnish with the remaining chives and serve.

Serves 4

Fish Curry

Hands-on time: 15 minutes
Cooking time: 25 minutes

1 tsp vegetable oil

2 onions, finely sliced

5cm (2in) piece fresh root ginger, peeled and grated

1 tsp ground turmeric

1 tsp ground coriander

1 tbsp medium curry paste

4 tomatoes, roughly chopped

400ml (14fl oz) fish stock

200g (7oz) raw peeled king prawns

300g (11oz) skinless white fish, such as cod, haddock, coley or pollack, cut into 2.5cm (1in) cubes

200g (7oz) frozen peas

salt and freshly ground black pepper

boiled rice or crusty bread to serve (optional)

1 Heat the oil in a large pan over a low heat. Add the onions and a good pinch of salt, then cover and cook for 15 minutes or until completely softened. Stir in the ginger, turmeric, coriander and curry paste and cook for 1 minute.

2 Stir in the tomatoes and stock and simmer for 5 minutes. Mix in the prawns, fish and peas, then cook for 3–5 minutes (stirring carefully to prevent the fish from breaking up) until the prawns are bright pink and the fish is opaque. Check the seasoning and serve with boiled rice or crusty bread, if you like.

Serves 4

Crusted Cod with Minted Pea Mash

Hands-on time: 10 minutes
Cooking time: about 15 minutes

50g (2oz) sun-dried tomatoes

2 tbsp sun-dried tomato oil taken from the jar, plus extra to serve

25g (1oz) grated Parmesan

4 skinless cod fillets

500g (1lb 2oz) frozen peas

1 tbsp extra virgin olive oil

a small handful of freshly chopped mint

salt and freshly ground black pepper

1 Preheat the oven to 200°C (180°C fan oven) mark 6. Put the sun-dried tomatoes, sun-dried tomato oil and Parmesan into a blender and whiz to make a thick paste. Alternatively, bash the ingredients together using a pestle and mortar.

2 Put the cod fillets on a non-stick baking tray and top each piece with a quarter of the tomato mixture. Roast in the oven for 12–15 minutes until the fish is cooked through and flakes easily when pushed with a knife.

3 Meanwhile, bring a medium pan of water to the boil and cook the peas for 3–4 minutes until tender. Drain. Put the peas into a food processor with the olive oil, mint and some seasoning. Whiz until the mixture is the consistency of a chunky mash. Serve immediately with the cod and a drizzle of the sun-dried tomato oil.

Serves 4

Understanding Nutrients

A quick and easy way to assess if a food is high or low in a particular nutrient is to use the table opposite. Look at the amount of a particular nutrient per serving or per 100g (3½oz) for snacks or cooking ingredients.

'We are what we eat'

From the moment of conception and throughout life, diet plays a crucial role in helping us maintain health and fitness.

A healthy balanced diet can protect against serious illnesses such as heart disease and cancer, increase resistance to colds and other infections, boost energy levels, help combat the stresses of modern living and also improve physical and mental performance. So, eating a diet that is healthy, varied and tasty should be everyone's aim.

Each recipe in this book contains under 300 calories per serving, and a maximum of 15g fat per serving.

Choose wisely

Our body needs over 40 different nutrients to function and stay healthy. Some, such as carbohydrates, proteins and fats, are required in relatively large amounts; others, such as vitamins, minerals and trace elements, are required in minute amounts, but are nonetheless essential for health. No single food or food group provides all the nutrients we need, which is why we need to eat a variety of different foods. Making sure your body gets all the nutrients it needs is easy if you focus on foods that are nutrient rich and dump those highly refined and processed foods that provide lots of saturated fat, sugar and calories but not much else.

	High	**Low**
Fat	more than 20g	less than 3g
Saturated fat	more than 5g	less than 1g
Sugar	more than 10g	less than 2g
Fibre	more than 3g	less than 0.5g
Sodium	more than 0.5g	less than 0.1g
Salt	more than 1.3g	less than 0.3g

Guideline Daily Amounts (GDAs)			
	Women	Men	Children (5-10 years)
Energy (cals)	2,000	2,500	1,800
Protein (g)	45	55	24
Carbohydrate (g)	230	300	220
Fat (g)	70	95	70
Saturated fat (g)	20	30	20
Total sugars (g)	90	120	85
Dietary fibre (g)	24	24	15
Sodium (g)	2.4	2.4	1.6
Salt	6	6	4

Moroccan Chickpea Stew

Hands-on time: 10 minutes
Cooking time: about 40 minutes

1 red pepper, halved and seeded
1 green pepper, halved and seeded
1 yellow pepper, halved and seeded
2 tbsp olive oil
1 onion, finely sliced
2 garlic cloves, crushed
1 tbsp harissa paste
2 tbsp tomato purée
½ tsp ground cumin
1 aubergine, diced
400g can chickpeas, drained and
    rinsed
450ml (¾ pint) vegetable stock
4 tbsp freshly chopped flat-leafed
    parsley, plus a few sprigs to garnish
salt and freshly ground black pepper
crusty bread to serve

1 Preheat the grill. Lay the peppers, skin side up, on a baking sheet. Grill for about 5 minutes until the skins begin to blister and char. Put the peppers into a plastic bag, seal and put to one side for a few minutes. When cooled a little, peel off the skins and discard, then slice the peppers and put to one side.

2 Heat the oil in a large heavy-based frying pan over a low heat. Add the onion and cook for 5–10 minutes until soft. Add the garlic, harissa, tomato purée and cumin and cook for 2 minutes.

3 Add the peppers to the pan with the aubergine. Stir everything to coat evenly with the spices and cook for 2 minutes. Add the chickpeas and stock, season well with salt and ground black pepper and bring to the boil. Reduce the heat and simmer for 20 minutes.

4 Just before serving, stir the chopped parsley through the chickpea stew. Garnish with parsley sprigs and serve with crusty bread.

Spicy Beans with Potatoes

Hands-on time: 12 minutes
Cooking time: about 1½ hours

4 baking potatoes
1 tbsp olive oil, plus extra to rub
1 tsp smoked paprika, plus a pinch
2 shallots, finely chopped
1 tbsp freshly chopped rosemary
400g can cannellini beans, drained
  and rinsed
400g can chopped tomatoes
1 tbsp light muscovado sugar
1 tsp Worcestershire sauce
75ml (2½fl oz) red wine
75ml (2½fl oz) hot vegetable stock
a small handful of freshly chopped
  flat-leafed parsley
grated mature Cheddar to sprinkle
sea salt and freshly ground black
  pepper

1 Preheat the oven to 200°C (180°C fan oven) mark 6. Rub the potatoes with a little oil and put them on a baking tray. Scatter with sea salt and a pinch of smoked paprika and bake for 1–1½ hours.

2 Meanwhile, heat the 1 tbsp oil in a large pan. Add the shallots and fry over a low heat for 1–2 minutes until they start to soften.

3 Add the rosemary and the 1 tsp paprika and fry for 1–2 minutes, then add the beans, tomatoes, sugar, Worcestershire sauce, wine and hot stock. Season with salt and ground black pepper, then bring to the boil, reduce the heat and simmer, uncovered, for 10–15 minutes. Serve with the baked potatoes, scattered with parsley and grated Cheddar.

SAVE TIME

For a quick meal that takes less than 25 minutes, the spicy beans are just as good served with toast.

Serves 4

Meat-free
Suppers

Iced Sweet Pepper Soup

Hands-on time: 5 minutes, plus chilling and freezing
Cooking time: 20 minutes

4 tbsp freshly chopped coriander
2 medium red peppers, seeded
  and sliced
1 medium onion, sliced
225g (8oz) ripe tomatoes, sliced
900ml (1½ pints) vegetable stock
150ml (¼ pint) milk
salt and freshly ground black pepper

1 First make coriander ice cubes. Put the chopped coriander into an ice-cube tray, top up with water and freeze.

2 Put the peppers into a large pan with the onion, tomatoes and stock. Bring to the boil, then reduce the heat, cover the pan and simmer for about 15 minutes until the vegetables are tender. Drain, putting the liquid to one side.

3 Whiz the vegetables in a blender or food processor until smooth, then sieve the purée to remove the tomato seeds.

4 Combine the reserved liquid, vegetable purée and milk in a bowl with salt and ground black pepper to taste. Cool for 30 minutes, then chill for at least 2 hours before serving. Ladle into chilled bowls and serve with the coriander ice cubes.

Serves 4

Broad Bean, Pea and Mint Soup

Hands-on time: 20 minutes
Cooking time: 30 minutes

1 tbsp olive oil

1 medium onion, finely chopped

1.1kg (2½lb) fresh broad beans (pre-podded weight), podded

700g (1½lb) fresh peas (pre-podded weight), podded

1.1 litres (2 pints) hot vegetable stock

2 tbsp freshly chopped mint, plus extra leaves to garnish

3 tbsp low-fat crème fraîche, plus extra to garnish (optional)

salt and freshly ground black pepper

1 Heat the oil in a large pan. Add the onion and fry gently for 15 minutes or until softened.

2 Meanwhile, blanch the broad beans by cooking them for 2–3 minutes in a large pan of boiling water. Drain and refresh under cold water. Slip the beans out of their skins.

3 Put the beans and peas into the pan with the onion and stir for 1 minute. Add the hot stock and bring to the boil, then reduce the heat and simmer for 5–8 minutes until the vegetables are tender. Cool for a few minutes. Stir in the mint, then whiz in batches in a blender or food processor until smooth. Alternatively, use a stick blender.

4 Pour the soup back into the rinsed-out pan, stir in the crème fraîche and check the seasoning. Reheat gently, then ladle into warmed bowls and garnish with a little crème fraîche, if you like, and a few mint leaves.

Serves 4

Warm Tofu, Fennel and Bean Salad

Hands-on time: 10 minutes
Cooking time: about 15 minutes

1 tbsp olive oil, plus 1 tsp

1 red onion, finely sliced

1 fennel bulb, finely sliced

1 tbsp cider vinegar

400g can butter beans, drained and rinsed

2 tbsp freshly chopped flat-leafed parsley

200g (7oz) smoked tofu, sliced lengthways into eight

salt and freshly ground black pepper

1 Heat the 1 tbsp oil in a large frying pan. Add the onion and fennel and cook over a medium heat for 5–10 minutes. Add the vinegar and heat through for 2 minutes, then stir in the butter beans and parsley. Season with salt and ground black pepper, then tip into a bowl.

2 Add the tofu to the pan with the remaining oil. Cook for 2 minutes on each side or until golden. Divide the bean mixture among four plates and add two slices of tofu to each plate.

Serves 4

Warm Salad with Quorn and Berries

Hands-on time: 5 minutes
Cooking time: 12 minutes

2 tbsp olive oil

1 onion, sliced

175g pack of Quorn pieces

2 tbsp raspberry vinegar

150g (5oz) blueberries

225g (8oz) mixed salad leaves

salt and freshly ground black pepper

1 Heat the oil in a frying pan, add the onion and cook for 5 minutes or until soft and golden. Increase the heat and add the Quorn pieces. Cook, stirring, for 5 minutes or until golden brown. Season with salt and ground black pepper, then place in a large bowl and put to one side.

2 Add the vinegar, 75ml (3fl oz) water and the blueberries to the frying pan. Bring to the boil and bubble for 1–2 minutes until it reaches a syrupy consistency.

3 Toss the Quorn, blueberry mixture and salad leaves gently together. Serve immediately.

Serves 4

Cherry Tomato Clafoutis

Hands-on time: 10 minutes
Cooking time: about 30 minutes

60g (2½oz) plain flour

1 tsp baking powder

3 large eggs

100ml (3½fl oz) semi-skimmed milk

3 tbsp shredded fresh basil, plus whole
  leaves to garnish

150g (5oz) cottage cheese

250g (9oz) cherry tomatoes

salt and freshly ground black pepper

green salad to serve

1 Preheat the oven to 180°C (160°C fan oven) mark 4. Put the flour, baking powder, eggs, milk and plenty of seasoning into a food processor and whiz until the mixture is smooth (alternatively, put all the ingredients into a large bowl and whisk together by hand). Empty the mixture into a bowl and whisk in the shredded basil and the cottage cheese.

2 Pour the mixture into a 1 litre (1¾ pint) shallow ovenproof serving dish, then drop in the cherry tomatoes. Season with ground black pepper.

3 Cook for 30 minutes or until the egg is golden and has set (a knife inserted into the mixture should come out clean). Garnish with basil leaves and serve immediately with a crisp green salad.

Serves 4

Perfect Peppers

Mediterranean vegetable fruits such as peppers
add a rich flavour to many dishes.

Peeling peppers

Some people find pepper skins hard
to digest. To peel raw peppers, use a
swivel-handled peeler to cut off strips
down the length of the pepper. Use a
small knife to cut out any parts of the
skin that the peeler could not reach.

Seeding peppers

The seeds and white pith of peppers
taste bitter, so should be removed.

1 Cut off the top of the pepper,
   then cut away and discard the
   seeds and white pith.
2 Alternatively, cut the pepper
   in half vertically and snap out
   the white pithy core and seeds.
   Trim away the rest of the white
   membrane with a knife.

1

Chargrilling peppers

Charring imparts a smoky flavour and makes peppers easier to peel.

1 Hold the pepper, using tongs, over the gas flame on your hob (or under a preheated grill) until the skin blackens, turning until black all over.

2 Put into a bowl, cover and leave to cool (the steam will help to loosen the skin). Peel.

Spicy Red Pepper Dip

To serve eight, you will need: 3 large red peppers (total weight about 450g/1lb), 200g tub reduced-fat soft cheese, ½ tsp hot pepper sauce.

1 Preheat the grill. Chargrill the peppers, as left, then peel and seed.

2 Put the flesh into a food processor or blender with the remaining ingredients and purée until smooth. Cover and leave to chill for at least 2 hours to let the flavours develop. Taste and adjust the seasoning if necessary.

1

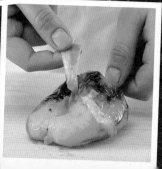

2

Mediterranean Stuffed Peppers

Hands-on time: 10 minutes
Cooking time: 35 minutes

2 Romero peppers, halved and seeded
75g (3oz) couscous
hot vegetable stock, to cover
50g (2oz) chopped dried apricots
finely grated zest and juice of ½ lemon
15g (½oz) chopped roasted hazelnuts
25g (1oz) pitted, chopped black olives
4 tbsp chopped mixed fresh soft herbs
25g (1oz) vegetarian feta
salt and freshly ground black pepper

1 Preheat the oven to 200°C (180°C fan oven) mark 6. Put the pepper halves into an ovenproof serving dish and roast in the oven for 25 minutes or until just tender.

2 Meanwhile, put the couscous into a bowl, just cover with hot stock, cover and leave for 10 minutes. Fluff up with a fork, then stir in the apricots, lemon zest and juice, hazelnuts, olives and herbs. Season with salt and ground black pepper.

3 Spoon the mixture into the peppers, crumble the feta on top and put back into the oven for 10 minutes. Serve warm or at room temperature.

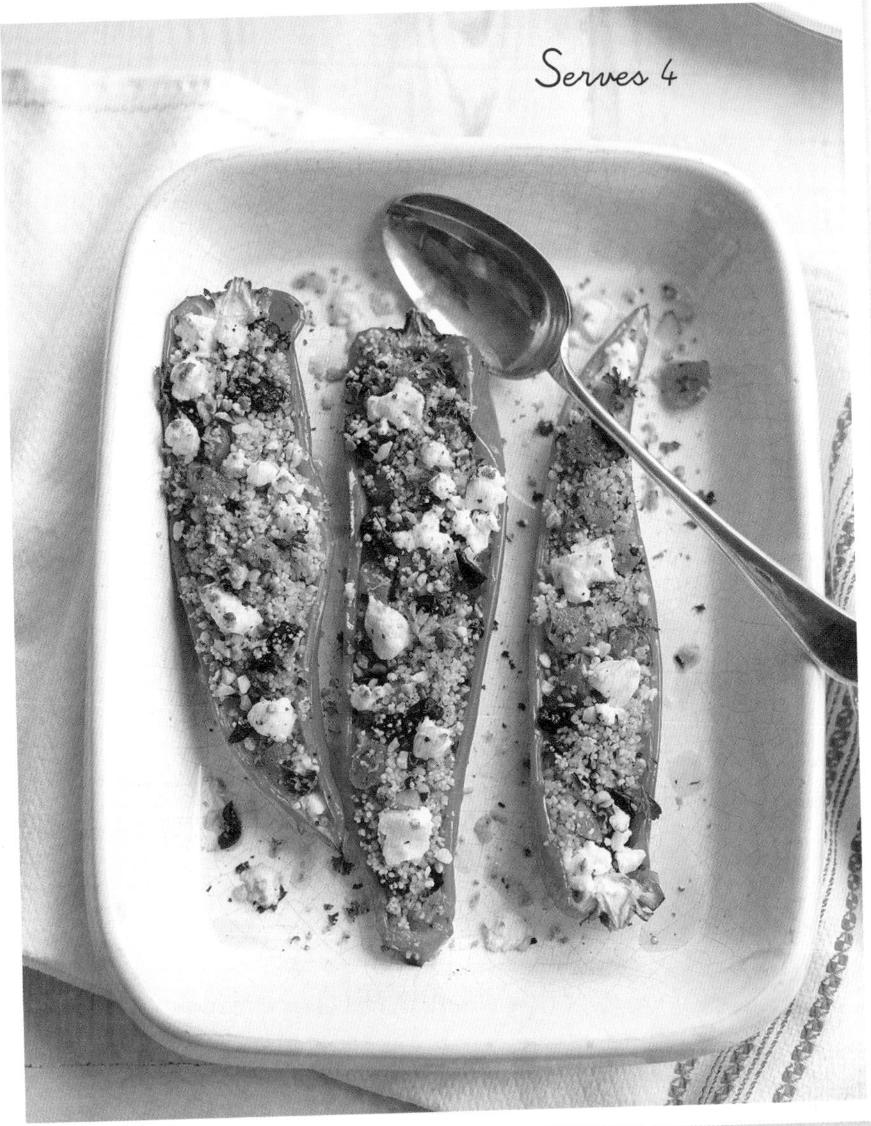
Serves 4

Veggie Bean Burgers

Hands-on time: 10 minutes
Cooking time: about 10 minutes

349g pack of firm tofu
2½ tbsp korma curry paste
4 spring onions, roughly chopped
a small handful of fresh parsley,
    roughly chopped
1 tsp paprika
1½ × 410g cans black-eyed beans,
    drained and rinsed
50g (2oz) fresh white breadcrumbs
½ tbsp oil
salt and freshly ground black pepper
salad to serve

1 Preheat the grill to medium and set the rack 10cm (4in) away from the heat source. Put the tofu, curry paste, spring onions, parsley, paprika and lots of seasoning into a food processor. Whiz until just combined, but not smooth. Add the beans and pulse briefly until they are roughly broken up. Tip the mixture into a large bowl.

2 Using your hands, add the breadcrumbs, then shape the mixture into four equal patties (squeezing together well). Transfer the patties to a baking sheet, brush with the oil and grill for 7–10 minutes until golden on top and piping hot. Serve immediately with a salad.

Serves 4

Stir-fried Vegetables with Oyster Sauce

🍴 **Hands-on time:** 15 minutes
Cooking time: about 10 minutes

175g (6oz) firm tofu

vegetable oil to shallow- and deep-fry

2 garlic cloves, thinly sliced

1 green pepper, seeded and sliced

225g (8oz) broccoli, cut into small florets

125g (4oz) green beans, trimmed and halved

50g (2oz) bean sprouts

50g (2oz) canned straw mushrooms, drained

125g (4oz) canned water chestnuts, drained

fresh coriander sprigs to garnish

For the sauce

100ml (3½fl oz) vegetable stock

2 tbsp oyster sauce

1 tbsp light soy sauce

2 tsp runny honey

1 tsp cornflour

a pinch of salt

1 First, make the sauce. Put all the ingredients into a blender and blend until smooth. Put to one side.

2 Drain the tofu, pat it dry and cut it into large cubes. Heat the oil in a deep-fryer to 180°C (test by frying a small cube of bread; it should brown in 40 seconds). Add the tofu and deep-fry for 1–2 minutes until golden. Drain on kitchen paper.

3 Heat 2 tbsp oil in a wok or large frying pan, add the garlic and fry for 1 minute. Remove the garlic with a slotted spoon and discard. Add the sliced pepper, broccoli and beans to the oil in the pan and stir-fry for 3 minutes. Add the bean sprouts, mushrooms and water chestnuts and stir-fry for a further minute.

4 Add the tofu and sauce to the pan and simmer, covered, for 3–4 minutes. Garnish with coriander sprigs and serve immediately.

Serves 4

Rich Aubergine Stew

🍴 **Hands-on time:** 25 minutes
Cooking time: about 30 minutes

1 tbsp extra virgin olive oil, plus extra
   to drizzle (optional)
3 medium aubergines, cut into 2.5cm
   (1in) pieces
1 onion, roughly chopped
2 celery sticks, roughly chopped
1 red pepper, seeded and roughly
   chopped
400g can chopped tomatoes
100g (3½oz) green olives, pitted
1 tsp caster sugar
1 tbsp red wine vinegar
a large handful of fresh parsley,
   chopped
50g (2oz) raisins (optional)
salt and freshly ground black pepper
crusty bread to serve

1 Heat the oil in a large pan and cook
the aubergines for 10–12 minutes
until brown and almost tender. Add
the onion, celery, red pepper and a
splash of water and fry for 5 minutes.

2 Add the tomatoes, olives and
some seasoning and simmer for
10 minutes or until the aubergine
is completely tender.

3 Stir in the sugar, vinegar, parsley
and the raisins, if using. Drizzle with
extra oil, if you like, and serve warm
or at room temperature with some
crusty bread.

Serves 4

Tomato and Butter Bean Stew

Hands-on time: 10 minutes
Cooking time: about 55 minutes

2 tbsp olive oil

1 onion, finely sliced

2 garlic cloves, finely chopped

2 large leeks, trimmed and sliced

2 × 400g cans cherry tomatoes

2 × 400g cans no-added-sugar-or-salt butter beans, drained and rinsed

150ml (¼ pint) hot vegetable stock

1–2 tbsp balsamic vinegar

salt and freshly ground black pepper

HEALTHY TIP

Butter beans provide good amounts of protein, complex carbohydrate, iron and fibre; they have a low GI so tend to release their energy over a longer period of time, keeping you feeling fuller for longer. They are also high in potassium, which helps to regulate fluid balance in the body.

1 Preheat the oven to 180°C (160°C fan oven) mark 4. Heat the oil in a flameproof casserole over a medium heat. Add the onion and garlic and cook for 10 minutes or until golden and soft. Add the leeks, cover and cook for 5 minutes.

2 Add the tomatoes, beans and hot stock and season well with salt and ground black pepper. Bring to the boil, then cover and cook in the oven for 35–40 minutes until the sauce has thickened. Remove from the oven, stir in the vinegar and spoon into warmed bowls.

Serves 4

Something Special

Piri Piri Chicken

Hands-on time: 15 minutes
Cooking time: about 45 minutes

1 red onion, cut into 8 wedges
1 tbsp olive oil
4 skinless chicken breasts
1 each red and yellow pepper, seeded
    and cut into strips
a large handful of fresh coriander or
    parsley, roughly chopped, to garnish
crusty bread, boiled rice or green
    salad to serve

For the sauce
1 red onion, roughly chopped
2 garlic cloves, roughly chopped
1 red chilli, seeded and roughly
    chopped
½ tsp smoked paprika
juice of 1 lemon
1 tbsp white wine vinegar
1 tbsp Worcestershire sauce
salt and freshly ground black pepper

1 Preheat the oven to 200°C (180°C fan oven) mark 6. Put the onion wedges in a medium roasting tin or ovenproof serving dish (just large enough to hold the chicken breasts in a single layer), add the oil and toss through. Put into the oven to roast for 15 minutes.

2 While the onions are roasting, make the sauce. Put all the ingredients into a blender and whiz until smooth. Put to one side.

3 Slash the top of each chicken breast to allow the flavours to penetrate. Carefully take the onion tin out of the oven, then add the chicken, sauce and pepper strips and gently toss everything together to mix. Rearrange the chicken in the tin, cut side up.

4 Cook for 25–30 minutes until the chicken is cooked through. Garnish with coriander or parsley and serve with crusty bread, boiled rice or a green salad.

Serves 4

Chicken Tagine

Hands-on time: 15 minutes
Cooking time: 25 minutes

1 tbsp vegetable oil

8 chicken drumsticks

½ tsp each ground cumin, coriander, cinnamon and paprika

75g (3oz) ready to eat dried apricots, finely chopped

40g (1½oz) raisins

400g can chopped tomatoes

75g (3oz) couscous

a large handful of fresh coriander, chopped

salt and freshly ground black pepper

1 Heat the oil in a large heatproof casserole. Brown the drumsticks well all over. Stir in the spices and cook for 1 minute. Add the apricots, raisins, tomatoes, 400ml (13fl oz) water and some seasoning. Simmer for 10 minutes.

2 Stir in the couscous and simmer for a further 5 minutes or until the couscous is tender and the chicken is cooked through. Check the seasoning. Sprinkle with chopped coriander and serve immediately.

Serves 4

Deluxe Fig and Ham Salad

Hands-on time: 10 minutes
Cooking time: about 10 minutes

200g (7oz) fine green beans, ends trimmed

3 tbsp extra virgin olive oil

4 slices white sourdough bread, cut into large cubes

4 little gem lettuces, quartered lengthways

85g pack of Parma ham

4 figs, quartered

1 tsp Dijon mustard

½ tbsp cider or white wine vinegar

salt and freshly ground black pepper

1 Bring a small pan of water to the boil and cook the beans for 4 minutes or until tender. Drain and leave in a colander to steam dry until needed.

2 Heat 1 tbsp of the oil in a large frying pan and fry the bread cubes, tossing frequently, until golden and crisp. Season with salt and leave to cool.

3 Arrange the lettuce quarters, cut side up, on a large platter. Roughly rip the Parma ham slices in half lengthways and weave among the lettuce quarters. Dot the figs, beans and toasted bread cubes over the top.

4 In a small jug, mix together the mustard, vinegar, remaining oil and some seasoning. Drizzle over the salad and serve.

Serves 4

Orange and Ginger Beef Stir-fry

Hands-on time: 10 minutes
Cooking time: about 8 minutes

1 tbsp cornflour

75ml (2½fl oz) smooth orange juice

2 tbsp soy sauce

1 tbsp vegetable oil

400g (14oz) beef stir-fry strips

5cm (2in) piece fresh root ginger,
   peeled and cut into matchsticks

300g pack of mixed stir-fry vegetables
   of your choice, chopped if large

1 tbsp sesame seeds

salt and freshly ground black pepper

egg noodles to serve

1 Put the cornflour into a small bowl and gradually whisk in the orange juice followed by the soy sauce to make a smooth mixture. Put to one side.

2 Heat the oil over a high heat in a large frying pan or wok. Add the beef strips and stir-fry for 1–2 minutes. Stir in the ginger, vegetables and a splash of water and stir-fry until the vegetables are just tender and the beef is cooked to your liking.

3 Add the orange juice mixture to the pan and cook, stirring occasionally, until thick and syrupy – about 30 seconds. Check the seasoning and sprinkle the sesame seeds over. Serve immediately with egg noodles.

Perfect Fish

Round fish include all those with a round body, such as cod, herring, mackerel and trout. Most fishmongers will prepare them for you but it is very simple to clean, bone and fillet them yourself.

Cleaning and boning

1 Cut off the fins with scissors. Using the blunt edge of a knife, scrape the fish from tail to head and rinse off the loose scales. (The scaled fish should feel smooth.)

2 Insert a sharp knife at the hole towards the rear of the stomach and slit the skin up to the gills. Ease out the entrails. Use scissors to snip out anything that remains. With the knife, cut along the vein under the backbone. Wash the cavity under running water.

3 Working from the belly side of the fish, cut along one side of the backbone, then remove as many fine bones as possible and separate the backbone from the flesh.

1

2

3

rn the fish over and repeat on
e other side of the backbone.
refully snip the backbone
th scissors, then remove.

Filleting

1. Using a very sharp knife, cut through the flesh down to the backbone just behind the head.
2. Working from the head end, insert the knife between the flesh and the ribs on the back of the fish.
3. Holding the knife flat on the ribs, cut all the way down to the tail until the flesh is completely detached along the full length of the fish.
4. Lift the detached portion of flesh and, with the knife again placed flat on the ribs, cut until the flesh is detached from the bones and remove the fillet.
5. Turn the fish over and repeat on the other side, again working from head to tail, to remove the second fillet from the fish.

Some cooks find it easier to remove the second fillet by keeping the fish with the unboned side down and working the knife under the ribs on both back and belly side of the fillet.

Cod with Oriental Vegetables

🍴 **Hands-on time:** 10 minutes, plus marinating
Cooking time: 6 minutes

4 thick cod fillets, each weighing 175g (6oz)

grated zest of 1 lime

1 tbsp chilli oil

1 tbsp sesame oil

1 red chilli, seeded and chopped

2 garlic cloves, chopped

8 spring onions, sliced

125g (4oz) shiitake mushrooms, sliced

225g (8oz) carrots, cut into strips

300g (11oz) pak choi, chopped

1 tbsp soy sauce

salt and freshly ground black pepper

lime wedges to serve

1 Put the cod into a shallow non-metallic dish. Mix the lime zest with the chilli oil and rub all over the fillets. Cover and leave to marinate in a cool place for 30 minutes.

2 Preheat the grill to medium-hot. Heat the sesame oil in a large frying pan. Add the chilli, garlic, spring onions, mushrooms and carrots and stir-fry for 2–3 minutes until the vegetables begin to soften. Add the pak choi and stir-fry for 1–2 minutes. Add the soy sauce and cook for a further minute. Season with salt and ground black pepper.

3 Meanwhile, grill the cod fillets under the hot grill for 2–3 minutes on each side until the flesh has turned opaque and is firm to the touch.

4 Pile the stir-fried vegetables on top of the cod and serve immediately with lime wedges.

HEALTHY TIP

Cod contains less than 1g of fat per 100g (3½oz) and practically no saturated fat. It is a good source of protein, vitamin B6, niacin, vitamin B12 and potassium. The carrots provide high levels of betacarotene, while the pak choi provides vitamin C.

Serves 4

Perfect Prawns

Prawns are ideal for stir-frying and quick braising, because they need very brief cooking, otherwise they will become rubbery in texture.

Peeling, deveining and butterflying

1. To peel prawns, pull off the head and put to one side. Using pointed scissors, cut through the soft shell on the belly side.

2. Prize the shell off, leaving the tail attached. (Add to the head; it can be used later for making stock.)

3. Using a small sharp knife, make a shallow cut along the length of the back of the prawn.

Using the point of the knife, carefully remove and discard the black vein (the intestinal tract) that runs along the back of the prawn.

4 To 'butterfly' the prawn, cut halfway through the flesh lengthways from the head end to the base of the tail, and open up the prawn.

4

Langoustines and crayfish

Related to the prawn, langoustines and crayfish can be shelled in the same way as prawns.

To extract the meat from langoustine claws, pull off the small pincer from the claws, then work with small scissors to cut open the main section all the way along its length. Split open and carefully pull out the flesh in a single piece. To extract the meat from large crayfish claws, crack them open using a hammer or lobster cracker, then remove the meat.

Also known as scampi, langoustines are at their best when just boiled or steamed, and then eaten from the shells. They can also be used in a shellfish soup.

Crayfish are sold either live or cooked. To cook, boil in court bouillon for 5–10 minutes. Remove from the stock and cool. Eat crayfish from the shell or in a soup.

Seafood and Lime Kebabs

Hands-on time: 15 minutes, plus marinating
Cooking time: 3 minutes

225g (8oz) raw peeled king prawns, deveined

550g (1¼lb) monkfish fillet, cut into 2.5cm (1in) cubes

juice of ½ lime

1 garlic clove, crushed

2 tbsp chilli oil

2 tbsp teriyaki sauce

2 limes and 1 lemon, each cut into 8 wedges

seeded and finely chopped green chilli, spring onion curls and fresh flat-leafed parsley to garnish

cooked rice noodles or boiled rice to serve

1 Put the prawns and monkfish into a bowl. Combine the lime juice, garlic, chilli oil and teriyaki sauce and pour over the top. Stir well to coat and leave in a cool place for up to 1 hour. Meanwhile, if using wooden skewers soak eight in water for 30 minutes.

2 Remove the seafood from the marinade and thread on to the skewers interspersed with lime and lemon wedges.

3 Heat a griddle or grill. Grill the kebabs for 3 minutes, turning once during cooking and brushing with the marinade. Garnish with green chilli, spring onion curls and parsley and serve with noodles or rice.

Perfect Mussels

One of the most popular shellfish, mussels take moments to cook. Careful preparation is important, so give yourself enough time to get the shellfish ready.

Storing mussels

To store fresh mussels safely, keep in an open bag in the fridge, covered lightly with damp kitchen paper (do not submerge in water for prolonged periods of time). Before use, check to make sure the mussels are alive – the shells should be tightly closed (give them a sharp tap on a work surface if they aren't, and discard any that haven't closed after 30 seconds or any that have broken shells).

Preparing mussels

1 Scrape off the fibres (beards) attached to the shells. If the mussels are very clean, give them a quick rinse under the cold tap. If they are very sandy, scrub them with a stiff brush.

2 If the shells have sizeable barnacles on them, it is best (though not essential) to remove them. Rap them sharply with a metal spoon or the back of a washing-up brush, then scrape off.

1

Cooking mussels

1 Discard any open mussels that don't shut when sharply tapped; this means they are dead and could be dangerous to eat.

2 In a large heavy-based pan, fry 2 finely chopped shallots and a generous handful of parsley in 25g (1oz) butter for about 2 minutes or until soft. Pour in 1cm (½in) dry white wine.

3 Add the mussels to the pan and cover tightly with a lid. Steam for 5-10 minutes until the shells open. Immediately take the pan away from the heat.

4 Using a slotted spoon, remove the mussels from the pan and discard any that haven't opened, then boil the cooking liquid rapidly to reduce. Pour over the mussels and serve immediately.

2

3

Smoky Spanish Mussels

Hands-on time: 25 minutes
Cooking time: about 20 minutes

2kg (4½lb) fresh mussels, scrubbed, rinsed and beards removed (see page 130)

2 tsp olive oil

1 onion, thinly sliced

2 red peppers, seeded and thinly sliced

1 garlic clove, thinly sliced

½ tsp smoked paprika

a pinch of saffron

500ml (17fl oz) fish stock

a large handful of fresh parsley leaves, chopped

crusty bread to serve (optional)

1 Sort the mussels following the instructions on page 130. Clean under running water, removing any barnacles or beards.

2 Heat the oil in a very large pan (which has a tight-fitting lid) over a medium heat. Add the onion and peppers and fry for 10 minutes or until softened. Add the garlic, paprika and saffron and fry for 1 minute more. Stir in the stock and half the parsley and bring to the boil.

3 Tip the sorted and cleaned mussels into the pan. Cover, reduce the heat and simmer, shaking occasionally, for 5 minutes or until the mussels have fully opened (discard any that remain closed). Divide among four large bowls, scatter the remaining parsley over and serve immediately with some crusty bread, if you like.

SAVE EFFORT

Try to buy rope-grown mussels – they're easier to clean.

Serves 4

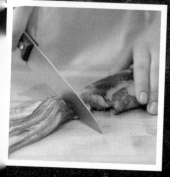

Preparing squid

Sliced into rings or cut into squares, squid is a popular fish in Chinese and South-east Asian cooking.

1 Cut off the tentacles just behind the 'beak'.
2 Pull out the beak and discard. Clean the tentacles well, scraping off as many of the small suckers as you can.
3 Reach inside the body and pull out the internal organs, including the plastic-like 'pen'.

4 Scrape and pull off the loose,
   slippery skin covering the body.
   Rinse the body thoroughly to
   remove all internal organs, sand
   and other debris.

5 Detach the wings and put to one
   side, then cut up the tentacles
   and body as required. To make
   squares, slice the body along one
   side, score diagonally, then cut
   into squares.

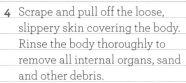

4

5

Squid, Pepper and Squash Salad

Hands-on time: 20 minutes
Cooking time: about 35 minutes

3 red peppers

1 tbsp oil

1 butternut squash (weight about 800g/1lb 12oz)

10 baby squid hoods (the white part), (total weight about 200g/7oz)

1 tbsp good-quality balsamic vinegar

100g bag of mixed leaves

15g (½oz) toasted pinenuts

a small handful of chives, roughly chopped

salt and freshly ground black pepper

1 Preheat the oven to 200°C (180°C fan oven) mark 6. Brush the peppers with a little of the oil and put into a roasting tin. Peel the squash and cut the flesh into 2.5cm (1in) cubes. Put into a separate roasting tin and drizzle ½ tbsp of the oil over them, then season with salt and ground black pepper. Roast the vegetables for 25–30 minutes, removing the peppers after 20 minutes or when slightly softened. Put the peppers into a polythene bag for 5 minutes – the trapped steam will help to loosen the pepper skin, making it easier to remove. When the squash is tender, take out of the oven. Cover with foil to keep warm.

2 Trim the squid and slice half into rings. Cut the remaining squid in half lengthways and lightly score one side with diagonal lines.

3 When cool enough to handle, peel the peppers, keeping any juices to one side. Discard the stalks and seeds and thickly slice the flesh.

4 Heat the remaining oil in a large non-stick pan and fry the squid for 2 minutes. Pour in the vinegar along with a splash of water. Add the squash, peppers and reserved juices and heat through. Check the seasoning. Serve on a bed of salad leaves with the pinenuts and chives scattered over.

Serves 4

Mushroom Roulade

Hands-on time: 20 minutes
Cooking time: about 20 minutes

250g (9oz) frozen spinach, thawed
4 large eggs, separated
freshly grated nutmeg
3½ tbsp cornflour
15g (½oz) butter
2 shallots, finely sliced
350g (12oz) mushrooms, sliced
400ml (14fl oz) skimmed milk
25g (1oz) mature Cheddar, grated
1 tsp English mustard
salt and freshly ground black pepper
green salad to serve

1 Preheat the oven to 190°C (170°C fan oven) mark 5. Line a 30.5 × 23cm (12 × 9in) tin with baking parchment. Squeeze out as much moisture as you can from the thawed spinach and put it into a large bowl. Stir in the egg yolks, nutmeg and plenty of seasoning.

2 Put the egg whites into a separate clean grease-free bowl and whisk until they hold stiff peaks. Quickly beat in 1½ tbsp of the cornflour, then fold the mixture into the spinach bowl. Empty on to the prepared tin, spreading it to the corners, then cook for 12–15 minutes until golden and firm to the touch.

3 Meanwhile, heat the butter in a large frying pan. Add the shallots and fry for 5 minutes or until softened. Increase the heat and add the mushrooms. Cook for 8–10 minutes until softened and any water in the pan has evaporated. Stir in the remaining cornflour, then the milk and heat, stirring, until thickened. Stir in the cheese and mustard. Check the seasoning.

4 Take the spinach base out of the oven and transfer with the paper to a board. Slide a palette knife underneath the roulade to loosen, if necessary, then spread the mushroom mixture over the top. Roll up lengthways as neatly as you can (don't worry if there's some spillage) and serve warm in slices with a green salad.

Tomato Risotto

Hands-on time: 10 minutes
Cooking time: about 30 minutes

1 large rosemary sprig
2 tbsp olive oil
1 small onion, finely chopped
350g (12oz) risotto (arborio) rice
4 tbsp dry white wine
750ml (1¼ pints) hot vegetable stock
300g (11oz) cherry tomatoes, halved
salt and freshly ground black pepper

To serve
fresh Parmesan shavings (optional)
green salad
extra virgin olive oil

1 Pull the leaves from the rosemary and chop roughly. Put to one side.
2 Heat the olive oil in a flameproof casserole, add the onion and cook for 8–10 minutes until beginning to soften. Add the rice and stir to coat in the oil and onion. Pour in the wine, then the hot stock, stirring well to mix.
3 Bring to the boil, stirring, then reduce the heat, cover and simmer for 5 minutes. Stir in the tomatoes and chopped rosemary. Simmer, covered, for a further 10–15 minutes until the rice is tender and most of the liquid has been absorbed. Season to taste with salt and ground black pepper.
4 Serve immediately with Parmesan shavings, if you like, a large green salad and extra virgin olive oil to drizzle over.

Serves 6

Puddings

Preparing Exotic Fruit

Sweet, fragrant exotic fruits are wonderful eaten raw but are also delicious in numerous desserts. Each fruit is unique and requires its own individual preparation technique.

Pineapples

1 Cut off the base and crown of the pineapple and stand the fruit on a chopping board.

2 Using a medium-sized knife, peel away a section of skin going just deep enough to remove all or most of the hard, inedible 'eyes' on the skin. Repeat all the way around.

3 Use a small knife to cut out any remaining traces of the eyes.

4 You can buy special tools for coring pineapples but a 7.5cm (3in) biscuit cutter or an apple corer works just as well. Cut the peeled pineapple into slices.

5 Place the biscuit cutter directly over the core and press down firmly to remove the core. If using an apple corer, cut out in pieces, as it will be too wide to remove in one piece.

2

3

Mangoes

1 Cut a slice to one side of the stone in the centre. Repeat on the other side.

2 Cut parallel lines into the flesh of one slice, almost to the skin. Cut another set of lines to cut the flesh into squares.

3 Press on the skin side to turn the fruit inside out, so that the flesh is thrust outwards. Cut off the chunks as close as possible to the skin. Repeat with the other half.

Exotic Fruit Salad

Hands-on time: 10 minutes

2 oranges

1 mango, peeled, stoned and chopped (see page 145)

450g (1lb) peeled and diced fresh pineapple (see page 144)

200g (7oz) blueberries

½ Charentais melon, cubed

grated zest and juice of 1 lime

1 Using a sharp knife, peel the oranges, remove the pith and cut the flesh into segments. Put into a bowl.

2 Add the mango, pineapple, blueberries and melon to the bowl, then add the lime zest and juice. Mix together gently and serve immediately.

Serves 4

Spiced Winter Fruit

Hands-on time: 20 minutes
Cooking time: about 20 minutes

150ml (¼ pint) port
150ml (¼ pint) freshly squeezed
  orange juice
75g (3oz) light muscovado sugar
1 cinnamon stick
6 whole cardamom pods, lightly
  crushed
5cm (2in) piece fresh root ginger,
  peeled and thinly sliced
50g (2oz) large muscatel raisins or
  dried blueberries
1 small pineapple, peeled, cored and
  thinly sliced (see page 144)
1 mango, peeled, stoned and thickly
  sliced (see page 145)
3 tangerines, peeled and halved
  horizontally
3 fresh figs, halved

1 First, make the syrup. Pour the
  port and orange juice into a small
  pan, then add the sugar and 300ml
  (½ pint) cold water. Bring to the
  boil, stirring all the time. Add the
  cinnamon stick, crushed cardamom
  pods and ginger, then bubble gently
  for 15 minutes.
2 Put all the fruit in a serving bowl.
  Remove the cinnamon stick and
  cardamom pods from the syrup,
  then pour the syrup over the fruit.
  Serve warm or cold.

FREEZE AHEAD
To make ahead and freeze,
complete the recipe. Tip the fruit
and syrup into a freezerproof
container and leave to cool, then
cover with a tight-fitting lid and
freeze for up to three months. To
serve, thaw overnight in the fridge
and serve cold.

Serves 6

Raspberry and Elderflower Jelly

Hands-on time: 20 minutes, plus chilling
Cooking time: about 10 minutes, plus cooling

8 sheets leaf gelatine
100ml (3½fl oz) elderflower cordial
500g (1lb 2oz) raspberries
75g (3oz) caster sugar

1 Wet a 900g (2lb) loaf tin, then line it neatly with clingfilm and put to one side. For the elderflower jelly, soak four of the gelatine sheets in cold water for 5 minutes to soften them. Meanwhile, put the cordial in a pan with 100ml (3½fl oz) water and heat until steaming, but not boiling. Take off the heat. Squeeze out the excess water from the gelatine, then add the softened sheets to the elderflower mixture and stir until dissolved. Pour the mixture into a jug, stir in 200ml (7fl oz) cold water and leave to cool completely. When cool, tip into the prepared loaf tin and evenly scatter 100g (3½oz) of the raspberries over. Chill for 2 hours or until just set.

2 While the elderflower jelly is chilling, make the raspberry jelly. Soak the remaining gelatine sheets in cold water as before. Put the remaining raspberries in a pan with 250ml (9fl oz) water and the sugar. Heat gently until the sugar has dissolved, then bring the mixture to the boil and bubble for 5 minutes, mashing the fruit as you stir until it's completely broken down and the mixture is fragrant. Strain through a fine sieve into a clean pan. Squeeze out the excess water from the gelatine, add to the raspberry mixture and heat gently, stirring until dissolved. Leave to cool completely.

3 Carefully pour the cooled raspberry jelly into the loaf tin over the just-set elderflower layer. Chill the jelly again until completely set – about 5 hours. When ready to serve, carefully invert the jelly on to a serving plate to unmould it. Peel off the clingfilm and serve in slices.

Baked Apricots with Almonds

Hands-on time: 5 minutes
Cooking time: about 25 minutes

12 apricots, halved and stoned
3 tbsp golden caster sugar
2 tbsp amaretto liqueur
25g (1oz) unsalted butter
25g (1oz) flaked almonds
low-fat crème fraîche to serve

1 Preheat the oven to 200°C (180°C fan oven) mark 6. Put the apricot halves, cut side up, in an ovenproof dish. Sprinkle with the sugar, drizzle with the liqueur, then dot each apricot half with a little butter. Scatter the flaked almonds over them.

2 Bake in the oven for 20–25 minutes until the apricots are soft and the juices are syrupy. Serve warm, with crème fraîche.

Serves 6

Apple and Blueberry Strudel

🍴 **Hands-on time:** 15 minutes
Cooking time: 40 minutes

700g (1½lb) red apples, quartered, cored and thickly sliced
1 tbsp lemon juice
2 tbsp golden caster sugar
100g (3½oz) dried blueberries
1 tbsp olive oil
6 sheets of filo pastry, thawed if frozen
low-fat natural yogurt to serve

HEALTHY TIP

This dessert is low in fat, as it is made with filo pastry (which contains virtually no fat) instead of shortcrust pastry (around 30g per 100g/3½oz). The blueberries are rich in anthocyanins – the pigment that gives berries their intense colour – which can help to prevent cancer and heart disease. Apples provide good levels of vitamin C and fibre.

1 Preheat the oven to 190°C (170°C fan oven) mark 5. Put the apples into a bowl and mix with the lemon juice, 1 tbsp of the sugar and the blueberries.

2 Warm the oil. Lay three sheets of filo pastry side by side, overlapping the long edges. Brush with the oil. Cover with three more sheets of filo and brush again.

3 Tip the apple mixture on to the pastry and roll up from a long edge. Put on to a non-stick baking sheet. Brush with the remaining oil and sprinkle with the remaining caster sugar. Bake for 40 minutes or until the pastry is golden and the apples soft. Serve with yogurt.

Serves 6

Summer Pudding

Hands-on time: 10 minutes
Cooking time: 10 minutes, plus overnight chilling

800g (1lb 12oz) mixed summer berries, such as 250g (9oz) each redcurrants and blackcurrants and 300g (11oz) raspberries
125g (4oz) golden caster sugar
3 tbsp crème de cassis
9 thick slices slightly stale white bread, crusts removed
low-fat crème fraîche to serve (optional)

1 Put the redcurrants and blackcurrants into a medium pan. Add the sugar and cassis and bring to a simmer. Cook for 3–5 minutes until the sugar has dissolved. Add the raspberries and cook for 2 minutes. Once the fruit is cooked, taste it – there should be a good balance between tart and sweet.

2 Meanwhile, line a 1 litre (1¾ pint) bowl with clingfilm. Put the base of the bowl on one piece of bread and cut around it. Put the circle of bread in the bottom of the bowl.

3 Line the inside of the bowl with more slices of bread, slightly overlapping them to prevent any gaps. Spoon in the fruit, making sure the juice soaks into the bread. Keep back a few spoonfuls of juice in case the bread is unevenly soaked when you turn out the pudding.

4 Cut the remaining bread to fit the top of the pudding neatly, using a sharp knife to trim any excess bread from around the edges. Wrap in clingfilm, weigh down with a saucer and a can and chill overnight.

5 To serve, unwrap the outer clingfilm, upturn the pudding on to a plate and remove the inner clingfilm. Drizzle with the reserved juice and serve with crème fraîche, if you like.

Serves 8

Perfect Sorbet and Granita

Sorbets have a fine, smooth texture and are most frequently fruit-flavoured.
Fruits vary in sweetness, so taste the mixture before freezing. Remove the
sorbet from the freezer 20 minutes before serving.

Simple Orange Sorbet

To serve six, you will need:
the finely grated zest of 3 oranges
and the juice of 6 oranges
(about 600ml/1 pint), 200g (7oz)
granulated sugar, 1 tbsp orange
flower water, 1 medium egg white.

1 Put the orange zest and sugar
   into a pan with 300ml (½ pint)
   water. Bring slowly to the boil,
   stirring, then reduce the heat
   and simmer for 5 minutes. Leave
   to cool for 2 minutes, then strain
   and cool completely.
2 Strain the orange juice into the
   syrup and add the orange flower
   water. Chill for 30 minutes.
3 Using an ice-cream maker,
   follow the manufacturer's
   instructions but remove the
   sorbet halfway through.
4 Whisk the egg white, add to the
   bowl, and continue churning
   until the sorbet is firm enough
   to scoop.

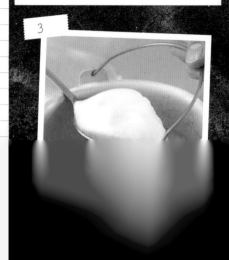

3

Granita

Granita is an Italian water ice with larger crystals than a sorbet. It isn't churned but is broken up with a fork, which makes it more like a frozen fruit slush. Quick to melt, it must be served and eaten quickly and makes a wonderful refresher in summer. Although normally made with fruit, granitas are also frequently flavoured with coffee.

Making by hand

1. Pour the mixture into a shallow container, cover and freeze for about 3 hours, until partially frozen to a slushy consistency. Beat the sorbet with a whisk or fork until smooth.
2. Whisk the egg white and fold into the mixture, then put back into the freezer and freeze until firm enough to scoop – about 2–4 hours.

2

Lemon Sorbet

Hands-on time: 10 minutes, plus chilling and freezing
Cooking time: 15 minutes, plus cooling

3 juicy lemons
125g (4oz) golden caster sugar
1 large egg white

1 Finely pare the lemon zest, using a zester, then squeeze the juice. Put the zest into a pan with the sugar and 350ml (12fl oz) water and heat gently until the sugar has dissolved. Increase the heat and boil for 10 minutes. Leave to cool.

2 Stir the lemon juice into the cooled sugar syrup. Cover and chill in the fridge for 30 minutes.

3 Strain the syrup through a fine sieve into a bowl. In another bowl, beat the egg white until just frothy, then whisk into the lemon mixture.

4 For best results, freeze in an ice-cream maker. (Alternatively, pour into a shallow freezerproof container and freeze until almost frozen; mash well with a fork and freeze until solid.) Transfer the sorbet to the fridge 30 minutes before serving to soften slightly.

Serves 4

Instant Banana Ice Cream

Hands-on time: 5 minutes, plus freezing (optional)

6 ripe bananas (weight about
  700g/1½lb), peeled, cut into thin
  slices and frozen

1–2 tbsp virtually fat-free fromage frais

1–2 tbsp orange juice

1 tsp vanilla extract

splash of rum or Cointreau (optional)

a few drops of lime juice, to taste

1 Leave the frozen banana slices to
  stand at room temperature for
  2–3 minutes. Put the pieces in a food
  processor or blender with 1 tbsp
  fromage frais, 1 tbsp orange juice,
  the vanilla extract and the liqueur,
  if you like.

2 Whiz until smooth, scraping down
  the sides of the bowl and adding
  more fromage frais and orange
  juice as necessary to give a creamy
  consistency. Add lime juice to taste
  and serve at once, or turn into a
  freezerproof container and freeze for
  up to one month.

Serves 4

Cinnamon Pancakes

Hands-on time: 5 minutes, plus standing
Cooking time: 15 minutes

150g (5oz) plain flour

½ tsp ground cinnamon

1 medium egg

300ml (½ pint) skimmed milk

olive oil to fry

fruit compote or sugar and low-fat
  Greek yogurt to serve

1 Whisk the flour, cinnamon, egg
and milk together in a large bowl
to make a smooth batter. Leave to
stand for 20 minutes.

2 Heat a heavy-based frying pan over
a medium heat. When the pan is
really hot, add 1 tsp oil, pour in a
ladleful of batter and tilt the pan
to coat the base with an even layer.
Cook for 1 minute or until golden.
Flip over and cook for 1 minute.
Repeat with the remaining batter,
adding more oil if necessary, to
make six pancakes. Serve with a
fruit compote or a sprinkling of
sugar, and a dollop of yogurt.

Serves 6

Rice Pudding

Hands-on time: 5 minutes
Cooking time: 1½ hours

butter to grease
125g (4oz) short-grain pudding rice
1.1 litres (2 pints) full-fat milk
50g (2oz) golden caster sugar
1 tsp vanilla extract
grated zest of 1 orange (optional)
freshly grated nutmeg to taste

1 Preheat the oven to 170°C (150°C fan oven) mark 3. Lightly butter a 1.7 litre (3 pint) ovenproof dish. Add the rice, milk, sugar, vanilla extract and orange zest, if using, and stir everything together. Grate the nutmeg over the top of the mixture.

2 Bake the pudding in the middle of the oven for 1½ hours or until the top is golden brown, then serve.

HEALTHY TIP

This comfort pud is a good source of protein and calcium, needed for maintaining strong bones. You can use semi-skimmed milk to reduce the fat content further.

Serves 6

Cheat's Chocolate Soufflés

Hands-on time: 15 minutes
Cooking time: about 12 minutes

butter to grease
75g (3oz) plain chocolate
225ml (8fl oz) fresh chocolate custard
3 medium egg whites
25g (1oz) caster sugar
icing sugar to dust

1 Preheat the oven to 220°C (200°C fan oven) mark 7. Put a baking sheet on the middle shelf to heat up, making sure there's enough space for the soufflés to rise. Grease six 125ml (4fl oz) ramekins.

2 Finely grate the chocolate, or whiz until it resembles breadcrumbs. Dust the insides of the ramekins with 25g (1oz) of the chocolate.

3 Mix the custard and remaining chocolate together in a large bowl. In a separate bowl, whisk the egg whites until stiff but not dry, then gradually add the caster sugar to the egg whites, whisking well after each addition. Using a metal spoon, fold the egg whites into the custard mixture.

4 Quickly divide the mixture among the prepared ramekins, put them on to the preheated baking sheet and bake for 10–12 minutes until well risen. Dust the soufflés with icing sugar and serve immediately.

Serves 6

107 cal ♥ 6g protein
4g fat (trace sat) ♥ 2g fibre
9g carb ♥ 1g salt

10

130 cal ♥ 7g protein
4g fat (1g sat) ♥ 1g fibre
18g carb ♥ 1g salt

12

157 cal ♥ 6g protein
4g fat (1g sat) ♥ 4g fibre
25g carb ♥ 1.2g salt

14

115 cal ♥ 2g protein
4g fat (0.7g sat) ♥ 3g fibre
17g carb ♥ 0.5g salt

20

234 cal ♥ 14g protein
9g fat (5g sat) ♥ 3g fibre
25g carb ♥ 0.4g salt

30

249 cal ♥ 10g protein
9g fat (4g sat) ♥ 1g fibre
31g carb ♥ 0.4g salt

32

221 cal ♥ 17g protein
9g fat (2g sat) ♥ 6g fibre
19g carb ♥ 0.9g salt

40

265 cal ♥ 37g protein
10g fat (2g sat) ♥ 3g fibre
5g carb ♥ 0.4g salt

52

161 cal ♥ 20g protein
7g fat (1g sat) ♥ 1g fibre
6g carb ♥ 0.2g salt

54

256 cal ♥ 29g protein
10g fat (5g sat) ♥ 6g fibre
14g carb ♥ 0.4g salt

56

232 cal ♥ 44g protein
4g fat (1g sat) ♥ 0.2g fibre
6g carb ♥ 0.4g salt

70

264 cal ♥ 13g protein
10g fat (2g sat) ♥ 0.8g fibre
30g carb ♥ 1.2g salt

72

274 cal ♥ 20g protein
9g fat (3g sat) ♥ 2g fibre
31g carb ♥ 2g salt

76

201 cal ♥ 28g protein
4g fat (0g sat) ♥ 4g fibre
15g carb ♥ 1.3g salt

78

294 cal ♥ 19g protein
13g fat (4g sat) ♥ 6g fibre
53g carb ♥ 1.3g salt

231 cal ♥ 6g protein
11g fat (5g sat) ♥ 2g fibre
30g carb ♥ 0.6g salt

296 cal ♥ 17g protein
10g fat (2g sat) ♥ 7g fibre
36g carb ♥ 1.7g salt

173 cal ♥ 14g protein
7g fat (2g sat) ♥ 3g fibre
13g carb ♥ 0.9g salt

223 cal ♥ 17g protein
2g fat (0.5g sat) ♥ 1g fibre
33g carb ♥ 0.8g salt

225 cal ♥ 45g protein
4g fat (1g sat) ♥ 1g fibre
3g carb ♥ 0.8g salt

209 cal ♥ 30g protein
8g fat (2g sat) ♥ 2g fibre
5g carb ♥ 0.2g salt

198 cal ♥ 16g protein
11g fat (3g sat) ♥ 2g fibre
10g carb ♥ 1.5g salt

122 cal ♥ 7g protein
7g fat (1g sat) ♥ 2g fibre
9g carb ♥ 0.3g salt

113 cal ♥ 12g protein
6g fat (1g sat) ♥ 3g fibre
1g carb ♥ 0.1g salt

202 cal ♥ 29g protein
5g fat (2g sat) ♥ 0.8g fibre
10g carb ♥ 0.5g salt

281 cal ♥ 37g protein
10g fat (3g sat) ♥ 0.8g fibre
10g carb ♥ 1.3g salt

232 cals ♥ 8g protein
9g fat (1g sat) ♥ 7g fibre
29g carb ♥ 0.8g salt

276 cal ♥ 10g protein
4g fat (1g sat) ♥ 7g fibre
56g carb ♥ 0.8g salt

72 cal ♥ 4g protein
1g fat (0.6g sat) ♥ 3g fibre
12g carb ♥ 1.3g salt

270 cal ♥ 37g protein
10g fat (3g sat) ♥ 6g fibre
12g carb ♥ 0.5g salt

239 cal ♥ 15g protein
10g fat (4g sat) ♥ 13g fibre
23g carb ♥ 0.8g salt

92

145 cal ♥ 9g protein
6g fat (0.8g sat) ♥ 5g fibre
14g carb ♥ 0.8g salt

94

122 cal ♥ 7g protein
7g fat (1g sat) ♥ 3g fibre
7g carb ♥ 0.4g salt

96

177 cal ♥ 13g protein
7g fat (3g sat) ♥ 1g fib
16g carb ♥ 1.3g salt

98

239 cal ♥ 12g protein
7g fat (1g sat) ♥ 13g fibre
32g carb ♥ 0.2g salt

110

271 cal ♥ 40g protein
7g fat (2g sat) ♥ 2g fibre
12g carb ♥ 0.8g salt

114

260 cal ♥ 17g protein
8g fat (2g sat) ♥ 3g fibre
33g carb ♥ 0.2g salt

116

192 cal ♥ 24g protein
5g fat (0.8g sat) ♥ 2g fibre
13g carb ♥ 1.2g salt

132

181 cal ♥ 12g protein
7g fat (1g sat) ♥ 5g fibre
19g carb ♥ 0.3g salt

136

168 cal ♥ 11g protein
9g fat (4g sat) ♥ 2g fibre
12g carb ♥ 0.5g salt

138

124 cal ♥ 2g protein
6g fat (2g sat) ♥ 2g fibre
16g carb ♥ 0.1g salt

152

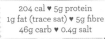

287 cal ♥ 1g protein
2g fat (trace sat) ♥ 2g fibre
60g carb ♥ 0.1g salt

154

204 cal ♥ 5g protein
1g fat (trace sat) ♥ 5g fibre
46g carb ♥ 0.4g salt

156

127 cal ♥ 1g protein
0g fat (0g sat) ♥ 0g fibre
33g carb ♥ 0.1g salt

160